In Search of Duende

LIFE ADVENTURES OF A CHEF

WRITTEN BY

Russell Dean Lowell

ISBN: 978-0-9915264-0-6-90000

Printed in the United States of America by LSC Communications

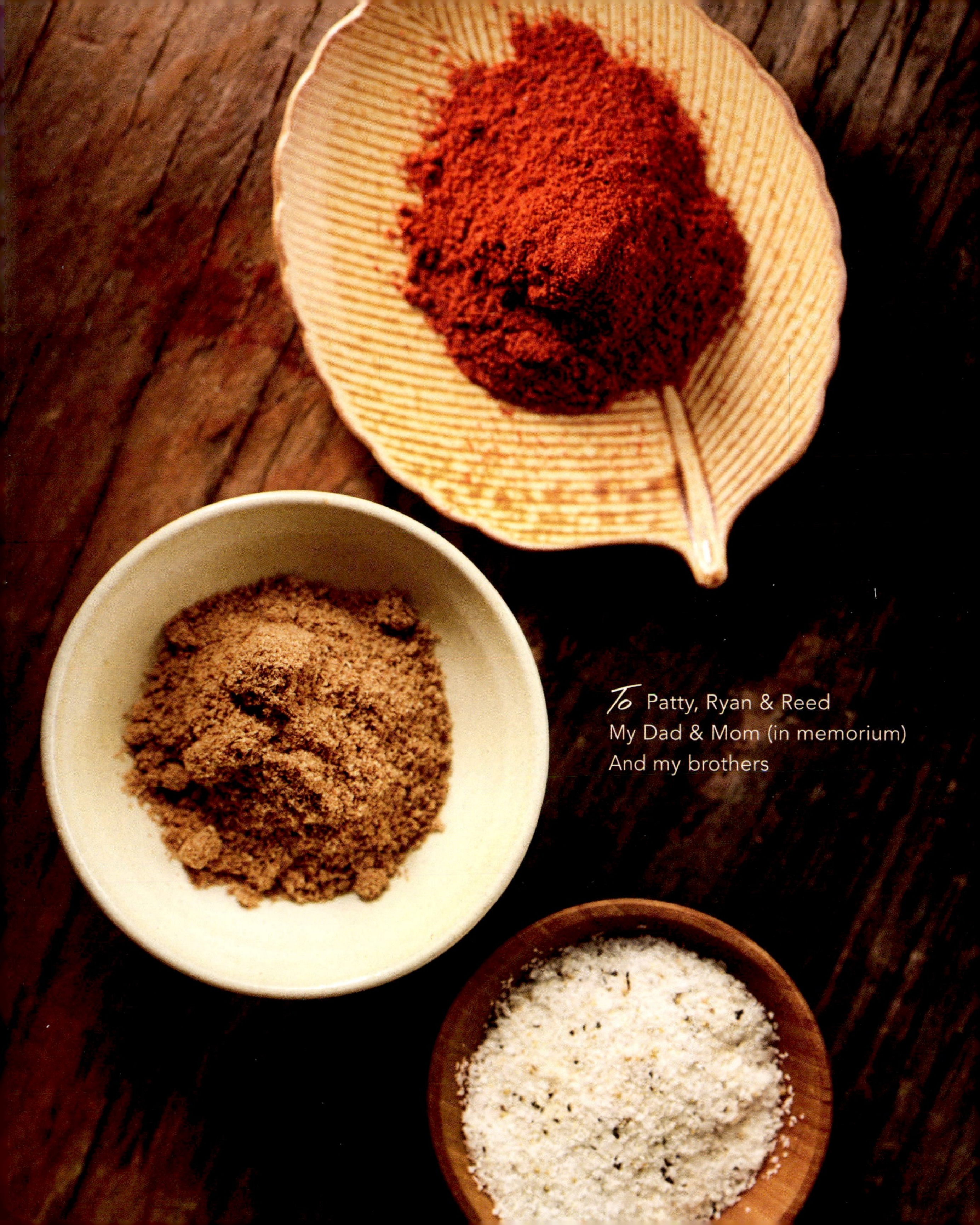

To Patty, Ryan & Reed
My Dad & Mom (in memorium)
And my brothers

Table of Contents

Introduction

A line cook once told me at the end of a long night, "Russell, you lead a charmed life." I laughed when he said it and I had to shake my head and disagree with him. I knew what he was trying to say but it wasn't quite right. I've always loved working hard and believed that ups and downs can become opportunities to learn new skills. But my fellow line cook was getting at something. That something is a perfect word the Spanish coined: *Duende*.

I have always been attracted to Spanish, being raised in Guantanamo Bay, Cuba as my dad was stationed there as a naval officer during the late 1960s. Spanish was in the air of my childhood even though the base is off on an isolated corner of Cuba, and Castro does his best to maintain that isolation.

After high school, I even studied Spanish at the University of Washington— not that I am any kind of scholar. I don't have the temperament, but I had enough dedication to write the papers, read the books. Mainly I just liked the language and I loved reading all the great poems: Lope, Quevedo, Juan Ramón, Darío, Neruda. Here's a poem I translated by the Cuban poet, Miguel Barnet:

THE PENCIL

My dear Pencil

Searching among the miscellaneous not all garbage

In match boxes with old telephone numbers,

School photos, papers and a faded yearbook,

I found you

There you were small and spent by my chewing

I have been delayed from turning back

I have returned to touch you

You're still the same, fragile tempered by my hands,

You have the same wooden pencil smell,

Of an empty desk, of interrupted day dreams

I can't seal you up again in that box

That weakened box

I simply can't close that desk

I have to write this poem with you.

I wish you were new again

I'll pull you from the dust my friend

Join with me key to my heart, you unspoiled beauty,

With the fool that will say anything

If someone happened to ask me the meaning of poetry

I would say that it's like you; yellow like young

Tender corn

And an indelible fragrance

Anyway, that special word: *Duende* (pronounced dwen-day). The Spanish use it to describe something real but hard to define, an extra something that intrigues and surprises. A person might be lucky or skillful but they also have that something extra, the Duende. A certain guitar player might have Duende, a player who can move a crowd a special way. Or a skillful matador might have Duende.

How about a chef? Why not?

A few years back, I was sitting in a pub in Issaquah waiting for a business associate to meet a couple to help plan a wedding. In the same section where I was waiting, three young women were playing darts. After a bit, they noticed me watching them.

"Come on over," one of the girls said. "Join us. Let's make two teams."

"No, sorry," I said. "I'm too good of a player."

At first, they seemed shocked and then they became intrigued. "What? What do you mean?" they asked. "Too good, really? Are you serious?"

I nodded. Now they really wanted me to play.

"Come on," they insisted. "Show us that you're not just BS-ing us."

I stood up, swaggered over to them, and faced the dartboard. I made a slight show of lining up my dart, squinting one eye. The young women looked at me and then at each other, casting doubtful glances.

I threw three bull's-eyes in a row.

"See?" I turned to them, "I tried to tell you I was too good."

I think my *Duende* was really with me that day; I had never played darts in my life.

In the meantime, my business pal had showed up. He played along and told the dart-playing ladies that I was a world champion…

Duende. A decent English translation might be "pixie." Duende has a tendency to bestow outlandish luck or a sense of being wowed. I suppose like everyone else I have leaned on the tried and true means to get through difficult life situations—faith, hope, prayer—but sometimes I do feel Duende on my shoulder—it comes upon me and then leaves again quickly. I even keep a small brown door around the restaurant to let my Duende come and go *(See photo)*.

My line cook was trying to point out to me that I fall into odd situations and come out, if not on top, at least not smothered and defeated. I will stick my head out of a mountain of garbage and a spring flower appears before me. In this book

I invite you to share some of these experiences with me. See what you think.

Speaking of Guantanamo Bay (since this is a book of memoires and stories, I want to share a bit about my childhood)—I think it does make up a big part of how I look at the world. As I mentioned, I was the son of an officer stationed at Guantanamo Bay, Cuba and one of four brothers. My dad was gone a fair amount. Since we lived in the environs of a closely guarded military fortification, my mom, more or less, let us run according to our whims. I think she was glad to get all us boys out of the house.

The accessible area around the base was underdeveloped, a tropical zone of mangrove so knotted that you couldn't tell where the water began or the jungle ended. The incoming tide filled long finger inlets that ran through marshes and banyan-covered forests, ending finally in mud flats. The pools and channels were perfect classrooms for my brothers and me. They were ready-made laboratories for kids willing and able to explore everything.

I can still picture myself, a nine or ten year old boy, sitting on the edge of a mangrove swamp. Don't be thrown by the word swamp. The salt water is very clear. Looking over the edge, you see red snapper, puffer fish, angelfish and parrotfish. They come flowing into the waterways, like flocks of birds, thirty or forty to a school, forming feeding patterns. I've never seen anything like that since, such brilliant, colorful schools planing in the water. I was usually alone. Now they are just memories...a kid...just watching...all within twenty minutes...a flash...what a show...gin clear water...and here comes a school of barracudas looking for something to eat!

In the eel grasses, everything was alive and moving: crabs, bait fish, sea horses and brine shrimp. You saw the hunger and activity of nature up close. In deeper waters you had barracudas, reef sharks, groupers, and spade fish. And the shells were scattered everywhere—in all varieties imaginable—triton's trumpet, king,

helmet, flamingo tongue, conch (all varieties) and coral (all kinds)—in rich and varied colors. It was a collector's dream.

It was a world of superabundant flora and fauna, and best of all, you got to touch it, or at least get close to it and test it with a child's curiosity. I have a memory that I treasure—so wonderful it seems like a dream— of being swamped and covered by a great swarm of Monarch Butterflies. Thousands of gold and black wings fluttering, searching for colorful plants and possibly attracted by my bright tee shirt, bunching and massing all over my body. It was glorious.

We didn't have much television compared to our stateside generation (one channel!) and radio wasn't really programmed for kids. The pull of nature and the outdoors was strong. And we ate everything! Roaming out and about on those sun-drenched days, it was a lot easier to eat what was on hand than hoofing it back to the house for a peanut butter sandwich. Easy to make a small stick fire where we could eat shellfish, fish of all kinds, and even spiny lobsters. Not even resident birds were safe from our rubber band guns. I believe this childhood set the stage that gave me the confidence to explore the terrains where I have lived with curiosity and enthusiasm.

I knew from high school that I wanted to be involved in the food world. I worked under a strict French-trained chef in San Diego. The lessons he taught me back then hold to this day: *Serve fresh food; take care of your guests.*

Introduction

When asked by a guest, "What should I order?" I always ask in return, "How would you like to feel?" This usually opens the door to a friendly dialogue in which I can tell a story which, in turn, lets me scope out what is the best fit for the guest.

I try to make people happy by serving the best food I can. That is what keeps me going. Often times I find out that the wheel has already been invented. That is when I break out a time-honored story and win them over.

What a great honor it is to take care of someone.

Let's say you are a young person, starting out in the food business. You are coming up through the ranks. Let's say you are the night cook and finishing your clean up. It is five minutes to ten and you are off at ten. Suddenly the door opens. A guest comes in and gives you a hungry pleading look. What do you do?

You say to the customer, "Whatever you want, I'm here for you." And you go ahead and make them anything they want. Technically, you're not being paid, but you take the time and tell yourself, *I can do this.* You make them anything on the menu that they want and make sure you take the time to say, "Hey, I can do that for you."

You have started the wheels in motion of my Shining Star Theory. You would be surprised what people will do when you treat them kindly. Very often, they do something kind back. Maybe they write a nice letter about you, maybe they will tell their friends about your place. *That guy is awesome. He did that. He met us past closing.* Nobody told you to do it but you did it because you wanted to make someone happy. You might not know what they are going through but you know that this will make them feel good. It makes them feel important. When no one else was around, when no one else could do it, you said, "yes."

Even today, I have many friends from those early days who still come around. "How do you want to feel?" I'll ask them when they give me that hungry look. Make the most of your opportunities. Be the one to do something for somebody, it will come back to you. Be the Shining Star.

So, what about that supposed charmed life that I lead? In reality, the glamour notes of a chef's life are few. We stand at least eighty percent of our chef-life, cutting meat, fish, guiding staff, etc. Call me right now if you don't believe me! I'll probably say, "I'm cutting meat. Got to go. Call you back."

Welcome to what follows: Duende stories, recipes, menus, friends, anecdotes and mostly fun…Enjoy—bon appetite!

The Halibut Story

Meeting famous people when they are without agents, managers, or publicists—they don't really seem famous. Thanks to my friend Chris Chelios I was able to meet many of them as just folks, in a setting where, again, they are people, friends of friends, relaxing and enjoying themselves. Their fame exists. It is there and it is interesting, but perhaps not the main thing. And you certainly don't want to make a big deal over it.

It was summertime, hockey season was over, everyone had finished doing what they'd been doing, school was out, and everyone met in Malibu. It was around nine o'clock at night, the kids were out running around, hanging off the balconies. Actually, you really had no idea where they were, but we—the adults—were out on the sand. The air was warm and the surf was loud. High tide, feet are in the water, it's gorgeous, and you're just happy to be where you are. People have beautiful sun-drenched tans and they're wiped out from the day's surf and sand, partying, smoking cigars, eating.

Laird Hamilton (surfer extraordinaire), Kid Rock, John Cusack, Patty Smyth, John McEnroe, Chris Chelios, me, and everyone else found ourselves sitting in the sand looking out at the ocean. The day was drawing to a fine close, things were getting mellow. Maybe a bit too mellow.

John McEnroe starts quizzing me about what I'm going to make for dinner tomorrow night. Everyone sitting around perks up, they know John likes to razz people. "What are you making tomorrow night, Russ?" he asked with a bit of edge in his voice.

I didn't feel like being razzed so I said without thinking, just to rise to the challenge: "Well, John, you see that boat offshore out there? Tomorrow I'm going out there on that boat and I'm going to catch a forty-pound halibut."

"No way man," John said. Everyone sitting around joined in and scoffed at the whole idea. *That's just Russell giving it back to John*, they were probably thinking.

I don't know who said it, but someone said, "No, man, this guy's a good fisherman. He travels with his rods."

Chris had chartered a fishing boat for us with a captain so I could go fishing while I was there. I had indeed brought my rods with me.

Patty Smyth said, "I'm going fishing tomorrow."

John Cusack said, "You know, what? I'm going with you, too. I want to learn how to fish from an expert."

The next morning, we were on the boat. The captain said, "I've got rods with me for everyone. Take your pick."

"No, no thanks," I told him. "I've got my own rods and I'm going to catch a forty-pound halibut today." The captain half smiled and said, "You know, you might be able to catch that where you're from, but you're not going to catch that down here."

"We'll see." I said.

I started off the day feeling fantastic. Patty Smyth is on the boat. She's a gorgeous brunette (I had a crush on her in high school) and she's singing Willie Nelson songs on the boat with her great voice. John Cusack is there too, setting up his rod with the captain. In a few minutes, I am all over the water, setting lines, watching, waiting. The sun has come up and starts to fry everything in sight.

About three hours go by and we're still waiting.

Oddly enough, I'm still feeling confident in my prediction of the day before. We have live bait, rods, the whole bit and still no bites. Lunch comes and goes and everyone starts giving me funny looks. *Maybe Russell is a bit cracked* their looks say. All day and no one is catching anything—not even a little garbage fish. I'm starting to feel the weight of the sun, the whole day on me.

At about five in the afternoon, I get a hit. I'm watching it carefully and then let some line out. I had a really light seventeen-pound leader on a steelhead rod. It wasn't made to catch halibut, but It was all I had with me at the time. At least it was a lucky rod though. Then I see the tip of the rod go down again, just slightly... tap, tap. *Well, okay*, I think, *we're onto something here.*

Cusack noticed. He said, "What do you think that is?"

"That's the halibut," I said confidently. "It's a forty-pound halibut, man! Watch!" In reality I was thinking: *How could I possibly know this is a halibut? I've caught halibut before and I've watched them. This could be any other fish.*

"I think you got the bottom, Russ." Cusack said.

"Oh yeah? Watch this." "ZZZZzzzeeeeeeeeeeeeeeeeee!" I set the hook, and the line made a terrific buzz as it slipped through the reel. Then it stopped.

Just as I'm holding the line, getting a little tension on it, here comes Kid Rock and Chris on jet skis. They come right up to the boat. I motioned for them to be quiet.

"Russ, what do you got?" Chris asked.

Again I motioned for them to be quiet. I said in a loud whisper, "I've got a forty-pound halibut on the line." He looked at me and gave me a look—a look I recognize—I've seen it quite a few times since we met so many decades ago. It says: *Come on, Russ, don't BS me.*

I ignored the familiar look. "Chris, this is a big halibut," I said. "We just can't see it. We're in about sixty feet of water so it's going to come up pretty fast when I start bringing it up. Right now it's just down there on a leash."

Chris just kept shaking his head and giving me the look. He tied up the jet skis and climbed on board with Kid Rock.

"Ok," I said. "This is what I'm going to need you guys to do. When I bring him up, I need you guys to gaff him. And you have to be really good and really quiet because when he starts to come up and sees the boat, he's going to go bat crazy."

I started bringing him up, just under the surface about five feet, with everyone looking over the side of the boat. The fish is just swimming, he's calm, he's not pissed off yet, nothing. He's just finning right there, just under the surface.

I said, "I'm going to bring him up close to the boat, so gently pull him over here and then you're going to gaff him". As soon as I did this, we gaff him and bring him into the boat.

Everyone gathers around, just standing there, staring at the halibut on the

floor of the boat. Something so ugly yet so beautiful. I won the lotto.

The night before, I had said to Laird, "Tomorrow is going to be Sunday and when I catch that halibut, I don't know if we're going to be able to get wasabi. Could you head over to the sushi restaurant and get some wasabi? We're going to need it for the sashimi." Laird agreed to do it.

Chris got on his cell phone from the boat and called Laird.

"Hey Laird, did you get that wasabi?"

"No. Did Russell get the fish?"

Chris yelled into the phone, "Laird, he got the fish!"

Laird jumped on his jet ski and came out to the boat. Chris held it up and Laird said, "Oh damn." He turned around and jets back to the shore to get the wasabi.

We headed back to the beach house.

John McEnroe was on the beach. He caught sight of the fish and yelled, "Oh my God!"

Everyone who was at our little beach soiree the night before, everyone who overheard McEnroe quizzing me about dinner, is floored. *How did you know you'd be able to catch that?* (It was not a forty-pound halibut—it came in at forty-eight pounds, according to the kids who "officially" weighed it using a bathroom scale.)

I laid that fish out gently on the picnic table as I looked at John McEnroe with a smile. Within a half hour, we were eating sashimi. The filets were beautiful, translucent white meat. Cusack was saying, "You're the man! He did it! I don't believe this! You are lucky, man. How did you know you were going to catch that fish?"

I said, "Well, I fish, I know they live here, we had live bait." As if that really explained anything. Right, Duende?

That halibut fed everyone for the next three days. We had grilled halibut fillets; we had halibut tacos and halibut ceviche, too. We had so much halibut it was coming out our ears. Catching that halibut was a bit like winning the lottery.

A good day of fishing, hanging out with friends, and eating a near magical halibut.

Grilled Halibut Tacos

1 pound fresh halibut

2 cups red cabbage,
shaved thin

2 cups napa cabbage,
shaved thin

½ cup green onions, chopped

½ cup lime juice

1 cup crème fraiche or
sour cream

½ cup cotija cheese

½ cup pico de gallo,
see recipe on prior page

8 small corn tortillas

Prepare a quick lime crème fraiche slaw: Stir lime juice into crème fraiche or sour cream, then toss with cabbage and green onion. Season to taste and set aside while grilling the fish.

Grill the halibut according to the recipe. Once cool enough to handle, gently flake fish into small pieces.

To assemble the tacos, warm the corn tortillas on the grill, layer on the fresh grilled halibut and cabbage slaw. Top with cotija cheese, pico de gallo and a squeeze of lime.

Grilled Halibut

Fresh halibut

Seasoning of choice or
Russell's Original Seasoning

Olive oil spray

Heat your grill until it is screaming hot. Season fish liberally with Russell's Original Seasoning. Spray the flesh of the fish with olive oil spray and grill for approximately three minutes on each side.

Pico de Gallo

Honey, to taste

1 Walla Walla sweet onion, diced

2 cups seeded Roma tomato concasse

½ cup roasted poblano chilies,
peel after roasting, seeded and diced

1 tablespoon white wine vinegar

1/2 bunch cilantro, chopped

2 garlic cloves, minced

1 teaspoon ground cumin

Juice of one lemon

Juice and zest of one orange

Prepare ingredients as directed, combine all and toss well. Marinate in the chiller for one day. Season to taste and toss again before serving.

Halibut Ceviche

For Halibut Ceviche, simply add one pound of fresh diced halibut and ¾ cup of lime juice to the pico de gallo recipe and marinate for four hours or overnight in the chiller. Serve with chips or just eat with a spoon.

Elk Camp

(EVERY YEAR IN THE FALL WE FEEL THE CALL)

Elk Camp is the hunter's refuge in a harsh wilderness setting where, next to food, adequate shelter is the priority. It carries many of its own traditions and has probably done so for as long as Native Americans and everyone else have been hunting on the North American continent. At elk camp, you dig in and see what nature has in store. You hope you possess skills that work: your life is dependent on absolute survival knowledge. One must be ready.

A modern day hunters' elk camp usually consists of a large and sturdy canvas tent, with some kind of cast iron stove for heat, (it takes four people to carry the stove from the truck) and an outside campfire not far from the tent. Inside the tent: a small dining table (maybe) and cots for each hunter. You want to have your tools ready: axes, hatchet, shovels, chainsaw, knives, and your arms of choice. The most important rule of any elk camp: make sure that you never enter camp with a loaded gun (or knocked arrow).

Above all, elk camp is a place to relax after exerting yourself after hiking or tracking in difficult terrain during an exhausting day's hunt. Hunting takes you far from cities and even small towns. (It goes without saying that there is no electricity and even cell phone use might be a luxury.) Coming into camp after a day of hiking and pursuing elusive prey, you want a comfortable and safe shelter. Just outside the tent, but not too close, you want a campfire where hunters can gather to cement camaraderie and trade stories of the adventures, exertions, close calls, and successes of the day. A good elk camp is a rewarding and important part of any hunt.

Welcome to Russell's Elk Camp.

Over the past twenty years I have taken groups of ten to fifteen guests into the Pacific Northwest wilderness to experience Russell's Elk Camp—a day-long, introductory version of a hunting elk camp that gives—I hope—my city friends a taste of the real thing.

The tent is set up and secured. Inside we've got a cast iron stove with its stovepipe running up and out the top of the tent. Instead of hunters' cots, we have set up dining tables with white linen and candle centerpieces. The guests arrive and it is fun to watch as they gain the sense of how removed from civilized comforts they are. The camp might be located at the end of an old logging road that takes

two hours to get to by four-wheel drive. I scout and choose the sites myself. Meanwhile, preparation for a luxury dining ex-perience is underway.

With both hunters' elk camp and Russell's Elk Camp, safety is primary. Trial and error in the wild can be deadly. I try to make most of my mistakes during hunters' elk camp so I can apply those lessons towards Russell's Elk Camp. But sometimes things just go wrong. One time four of us spent about three hours setting up the tent and stove for Russell's Elk Camp. The guests arrived and it started to snow. They had a great time and everyone thought the snow added a realistic touch to the camp. We finished camp and the staff and I went to see the guests off at the trailhead. We came back ready to strike camp and found our tent half sunk in snow. A couple old growth cedars above the tent had grown together forming a catcher's mitt in the crown of the trees where it caught a huge pile of snow. It gave way and released a couple thousand pounds of snow upon our tent burying the canvass and bending support poles.

On another occasion, we were on our way to set up elk camp. One of our group had spotted a herd of elk on the way in. We were so eager to do some reconnaissance that we arrived and did the minimum of camp setup, thinking we would finish up later. When we came back, it was getting towards evening and the wind started up in a big way. We were still setting up camp in the dark with all of our mistakes revealed: we hadn't dug in, we hadn't staked the tent, and we hadn't secured the tent stovepipe. In our absence, a high mountain storm had kicked up. It was all we could do to keep the tent from blowing away in forty-knot winds. Whether setting up hunters' elk camp or Russell's Elk Camp, you have to take it seriously and constantly think of safety. Either way, elk camp is a unique experience.

We might set up Russell's Elk Camp within striking distance of a sheer rock face with sparse vegetation that blends into a heavily wooded saddle. In the distance you might hear the swish of a stream or the bugle call of an elk. The crew arrives early and the guests arrive by noon and start in on hors d'oeuvres and drinks or beverages. They begin to relax; they are enjoying themselves seated amid wilderness grandeur that most have only observed from an airplane. They might look up on the ridge and see a mountain goat with black horns leaping from a rock face. Or further out, alongside an outcropping with light vegetation, we might spot a bull

elk working his way like a patient rock climber cutting a diagonal path of his own making. More often, a doe might sniff us out and we spot her bounding into the ravine below. The guests are thrilled to be out in authentic Washington State wilderness.

It's time for dinner. There are, say, twelve guests, and I'll seat them inside the tent at tables with white linens,

Chef Grant Achatz of Alinea in Chicago

china, and candlelight. Add Johnny Cash, wild game, usually elk or filet mignon. (Even Don Julio has been to Elk Camp.) This will be followed by a second and third course of pan fried trout, quail, or whatever I feel best fits the occasion (Wild boar, quail, duck, or pheasant). All the dishes should have an in-the-wild theme.

Being surrounded by the rugged ranges and peaks of the Cascade Mountains brings out a great combination of amazement and happiness in my guests. People love eating and drinking in the wild. The smell of wood smoke brings out good memories. Guests love checking on the wood stove and keeping it fed. Sometimes the men will want to chop kindling and I'll say go for it. Sometimes the women will want to smoke cigars. Have one on me. Elk camp is just plain fun—guests don't want to leave, and neither do I!

Often, after a Russell's Elk Camp, I'll arrive back at the restaurant to help put the dinner rush out. I am back in the reality of working the line in the kitchen. My line cooks will look at me and I know they are wondering, *What is this guy doing here? He's been going since four o'clock this morning and we've got to get up tomorrow and do it again on Sunday.* The whole feeling of elk camp is still with me and I'm still feeling incredibly energized.

During one elk camp, we had a group of Japanese businessmen on a visit to a famous software company in our area. The head of said software company specifically asked me to make sure the Japanese visitors had a good time. After dessert, we still had about one hour of light left. Out of the blue, one of the Japanese executives asked me, "Do you have any guns around?"

As a matter of fact, I did. I had a 300 H&H magnum and a 30.06 Winchester. We set up a shooting range. I also happened to have a few cowboy hats in the back of my truck and I fixed them on the Japanese execs. We blew through a couple hundred dollars' worth of ammo and they loved it. Later I found out the software company closed the deal with the Japanese.

At another Elk Camp, a famous local food writer accompanied a group who had bid on the camp as a charitable donation to Fred Hutchison Cancer Research Center. I was up in a tree photographing guests arriving when the group arrived. The famous local food writer asked where I was. One of the wait staff told her that earlier a cougar had come around and tore up camp a bit, that Russell had grabbed his bow, and we haven't seen him since. They pointed her towards the trail where my tree was planted. She followed a trackless fresh powder path that meandered down to a little creek. Old growth cedar trees and hemlock on either side. She must have been feeling brave since she headed down the trail. From up in the tree I watched her walk past my tree for about twenty feet. I waited until she passed by my high hide (tree stand) and let out a near perfect imitation of a mountain lion howl. Guuurrroowl! She took off running unaware that it was me and not a wild animal. The famous local food writer ran back to the campsite, obviously scared out of her wits. Everyone laughed.

I arrived a few minutes later laughing and thinking *well, there goes a good review of Russell's Elk Camp*. We had a great main course of elk medallions with a superb wine. After dinner, we shot bows and arrows. As it turned out our food writer gave us a good review. (Thank you very much!)

We have continued to hold Russell's Elk Camps every year since then. Holding the camps in winter months, we have been very fortunate: we have never gotten snowed in; we have never been caught in a blizzard, flood, or an avalanche; we've never been attacked by wild animals—though many often pass right by our tent.

I am most proud that, thanks to over one hundred Russell's Elk Camps, held over the past twenty years, we have been able to help raise thousands of dollars for charity. Many of the camps are bid on at charity auction events and they often render high donations. One of the recipients I cherish most is the Fred Hutchinson Cancer Research Center.

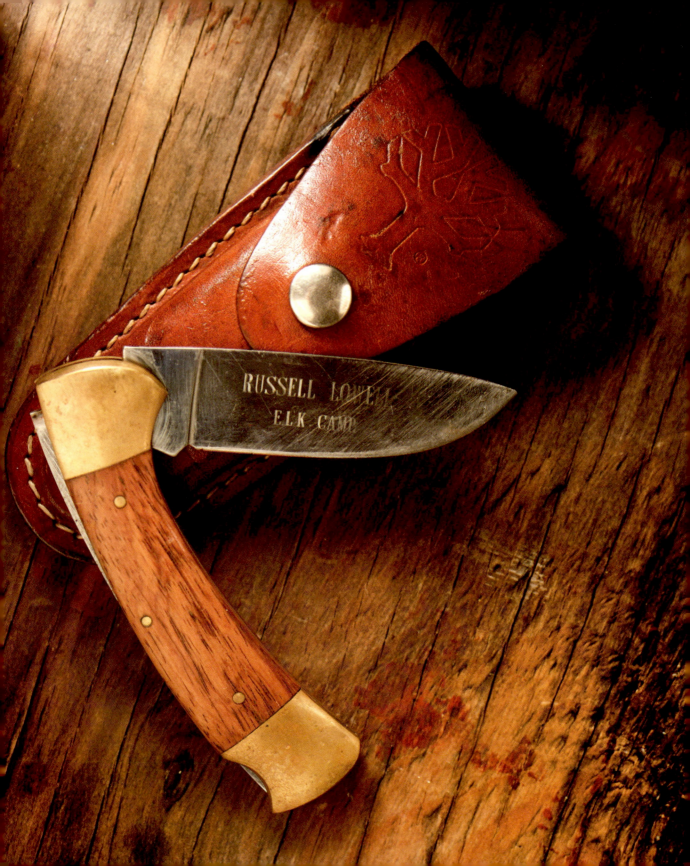

Elk Camp

SALAD
Warm Forest Mushroom & Belgian Endive Salad
with Goat Cheese & Thyme Vinaigrette

PASTA
Open Faced Braised Pheasant Ravioli with Celeriac Purée,
Pearl Onions & Truffle Butter Sauce

ENTRÉE
Roast Elk Loin with Chorizo, Pearl Barley Risotto,
Sautéed Greens & Smoked Paprika Nage

DESSERT
Raisin Pecan Bread Pudding
with Warm Calvados Cream & Stewed Winter Fruit

Elk Roast with Caramelized Onions & Wild Mushrooms

24 oz. elk roast

1 chopped Walla Walla onion

3 cloves garlic

Bay leaf

Black peppercorn

3 sprigs fresh thyme

1 cup red wine

32 oz. veal stock/beef stock

2 tablespoons butter

Wild mushrooms

1 chopped Walla Walla onion

ELK ROAST

Preheat oven to 300 degrees. In an oven safe pot, sear elk until browned on all sides. Add onion, garlic, bay leaf, peppercorn, thyme and red wine. Cook for two minutes and then add the veal stock. Cover with a lid or foil and put in the oven for 45 minutes to an hour. Pull out of oven, rest meat on a tray and reduce braising liquid until nape *(thick enough to coat the back of a spoon without running off)*. Strain the liquid and whisk in butter. Hold sauce on low heat. Slice roast one inch thick on a bias.

CARAMELIZED ONIONS & WILD MUSHROOMS

Slice onion and sauté on medium/low heat until caramelized, about ten minutes. Turn up the heat to a med/high and add the mushrooms. Sauté mushrooms for three minutes.

Serve the sliced elk on caramelized onions and wild mushrooms and top with veal demi-glace.

Pink Apron

MARILYN LOWELL, IN MEMORIUM

Here I am in a pink apron. The whole pink apron thing came about because of my cooking classes. Anyone who came to the classes got a free apron. I would print out the recipe card and hand them out and I did it all for free. Men would get teal colored aprons (with a quail sewn on the pocket) and the women pink aprons. My mother actually made the aprons, hand stitching them all. All the students loved their aprons. Some even sent aprons back saying thanks and wanting to keep the good vibes going.

Mom was incredibly talented with her hands, she could make anything—knitting crochet, quilts, embroidery, sewing you name it. She even made Barbie Doll clothes! She also knew about herbs and gardening. She was a great person to learn from. She always had something interesting to say. Even after she got sick, she was still going, especially with her herb garden.

My mother got cancer and as a part of thinking about her every day during that hard time, I wore one of the pink aprons that she made. During the time my mom was really sick, I would wear a pink apron every night.

Later on, I found a box of pink aprons. I started wearing one regularly at my restaurant, Russell's. I would go out on the floor to greet my guests and they would always comment on the pink apron. Later on, I noticed they even began disappearing from the laundry. I couldn't believe it. People tracked it to that degree? Time went by and I became known for the pink apron. I didn't push it but I wanted to do something to heighten awareness of cancer research and do it for my mom above all.

RICK BAYLESS TWEET

"Gr8 nite! U&ur crew r the best! RT Finishing up spectacular nite w Chef Bayless 2 benefit Fred Hutch Cancer Research Ctr."

Fred Hutchinson Cancer Research Center

Fred Hutchinson Cancer Research Center is a world leader in cancer and disease research. Their work is at the center of revolutionary discoveries, better treatments, and healthier lives. They believe that working together is the fastest way to discover cures and honor the courage of patients, the compassion of caregivers, and the belief in a disease-free future.

Fred Hutch's annual Premier Chefs Dinner is a four-course, $250-a-plate extravaganza prepared by the Northwest's top chefs for over twenty years. Since the inaugural dinner, the evening and auction have raised about $5.5 million to support research at Fred Hutch. Russell has been involved with the Hutch for over twenty years.

In 2013, Chef Rick Bayless attended the Premier Chefs Dinner as the guest speaker. Russell invited him to fly back to Seattle and cook dinner with him for guests who bought tickets at the auction. In October, Chef Lowell & Chef Bayless co-hosted 110 guests with both chefs providing their own touches to the dinner. This event raised a large amount of money for cancer research.

Marilyn's Stuffed Chicken Breast

1 cup celery - diced

1 cup onions - diced

3 eggs, lightly beaten

6 cups bread, torn

2 cups chicken stock

Russell's Original

Seasoning, to taste

1 teaspoon, fresh thyme

4 ounces unsalted butter, melted

1 teaspoon, fresh chopped parsley

1 teaspoon baking powder

½ cup dried cranberries

1-2 tablespoons olive oil

4 - 8 ounce airline

chicken breasts

Russell's Original Seasoning

STUFFING

Dice celery, onion and bread. Combine chopped parsley, thyme, dried cranberries, celery, onion, chicken stock, Russell's original seasoning, eggs and butter. Toss and add baking powder. Toss again and set aside.

Preheat oven to 350 degrees

CHICKEN BREAST

On the opposite side of the chicken wing, make a cut down the side creating a pocket. The cut should be even on both sides, approximately two to three inches deep and three inches long. Heat oven safe sauté pan with one to two tablespoons of olive oil. Place stuffed chicken skin side up. Season skin liberally and place in oven for approximately twenty-five minutes or until golden brown.

The Purple Barer

Stan Barer has been a good friend to me for many years. Stan's can-do attitude towards life and everything about him has inspired me to exceed my own expectations.

It is impossible to try to press his many achievements in law, business, and philanthropy into a few paragraphs but here goes. A capsule view might go like this:

Stan Barer was born and raised in Eastern Washington and after college worked as a legislative aide to Warren Magnuson, Washington State's powerful US senator who moved the state to the forefront of defense and health sciences research in the decades after World War II. As a young lawyer, he helped formulate legislation that expanded American trade internationally while protecting American workers. His subsequent career is notable for achievements in business, law and trade. As a founder of the Washington State China Relations Council, Stan has played a key role in helping Washington State benefit from China's rise as a world power and into one of America's biggest trading partners. The political legal business and cultural relationships Stan has developed with China will continue to bear fruit for many years to come.

Stan is retired now but he can look back on his accomplishments and see that they have expanded in positive ways. With his wife Alta, Stan has been instrumental in public service and charitable work...the University of Washington School of Law...the Fred Hutchinson Cancer Research Center...his charitable work extends to many under-the-radar folks and organizations. (He asked me not to mention some of these so I'll claim modesty as a trait on his behalf.)

Almost all of the foregoing I learned after coming to know Stan as a personable and engaging man. He also has great competitive drive; sometimes I see flashes that give me a hint about his success in so many areas of life.

For example, on a recent fly-fishing trip, we found ourselves—six fly fishermen pals, including Stan and me—out on the Salmon River in Idaho. We all stood within talking distance of each other along the riverbank but Stan was a few feet out, wearing waders. He was casting with the Purple Barer. Named in his honor, it was a fly I had tied using the fan colors of the University of Washington Huskies (Stan's Alma Mater).

It was the last day of the last fish and Stan had thrown his final cast. Everyone was getting ready to wrap up, putting rods and tackles away when Stan gave one final cast. He got a hit. Just like that. The fish jumped. He was huge—a lovely silver steelhead rising wonderfully out of the water. All the other fishermen had caught something

Stan Barer (on right) with his guide JT on the Salmon River

that day but nothing this big. Again, we glimpse him as he is jumping out of the water and we can't believe it. The fight it is on. With a fish this big you've got to be careful, he can pull away or snap the line just like that. It requires finesse to pull him in. The rod is taxed, the drag is set, and Stan is moving with it, struggling slightly but letting it run in and out, showing us that he has

still got it. As we had already seen, it's big. Our fellow fly fishermen began shouting out all kinds of advice:

Hold on!

Tip up!

Your drag is too loose!

Ease up!

Get the net!

Stan has got it securely on the line and the other fishermen are still yelling directions at him. The more they yelled the more it seemed—to me—like something out of the novel, *The Lord of the Flies*. In a weird way, the more they shout maybe the more they want him to lose the fish. Everyone gets so competitive and intense; time seems to stand still.

Stan stays with it and finally the fish tires out; he is bringing to hand—with no net—a beautiful, rainbow-sheened, 31.5 inch steelhead. Just think: that fish had swum over six hundred miles to get back to its spawning ground. Stan let him out gently back into the river.

Afterwards, our fly-fishing group asked me for any spare fly samples…

Stan is a family man of great humor and energy. Both he and his wife, Alta enjoy connecting with people of varying backgrounds and interests, from associates in business, diplomatic or political circles to scholarship students. He and Alta enjoy the opportunity to host events and dinners in Seattle or retreat locations around the Pacific Northwest. I enjoy being a part of their generous hospitality. During the 2008 presidential primary season, Stan asked me to prepare dinner for guests who would be celebrating Hillary Clinton's Birthday. He even asked me to bake a chocolate cake for her.

The day arrived and everything was going great. We had prepared pan-seared sea bass and wild mushroom risotto. For dessert, I made a special large chocolate raspberry cake. I was standing in the back of the kitchen when four guys in suits and dark sunglasses approached me and told me that I would have to cut the cake up before Mrs. Clinton cut into it.

STAN BARER

Stan Barer was the Senate lawyer for the landmark 1964 Civil Rights act provisions that created the right for all regardless of race to be served in public accommodations such as restaurants and hotels. His legal reasoning and report on the provisions were relied upon by the US Supreme Court in upholding the Act.

Stan developed a legal theory that was adopted by the US Attorney General that reversed the prohibition—in effect since the Korean War—that prevented ships and planes owned by the People's Republic of China to engage in commercial service to the United States. So in April of that year, the first vessel flying the flag of the People's Republic of China came to the US and its destination was Seattle.

I just nodded and didn't say anything to them. I found Stan and told him, "I think the secret service wants me to cut the cake before Hillary slices into it.

"I'll take care of it," Stan said. (I believe he wanted eight candles on the cake—four candles in each half to represent the years of Mrs. Clinton's two presidential terms. A loyal—and optimistic supporter, he.)

After dinner, Stan poked through the kitchen door and said, "Everything's OK. Don't cut into the cake just yet. You're in the clear. Just be ready to bring it out in five minutes."

Five minutes later, dodging through the crowd, I'm carrying a tray with the large chocolate cake. Stan is at the microphone addressing the crowd of hundreds of people. Just as I finished setting down the tray with the cake on it, I hear him say, "And now our Republican chef would like to sing 'Happy Birthday' to Hillary Clinton." He shoves the microphone at my nose. I grab it and find myself singing Happy Birthday to Hillary Clinton.

I can't believe I just sang Happy Birthday to Hillary Clinton.

Only the laughter and applause of the guests told me that I really did do that and I think Stan Barer was laughing and clapping harder than anyone.

Hillary Clinton Birthday Celebration 2007

PASSED HORS D'OEUVRES
Shaved Lamb with Caramelized Onion & Balsamic Reduction
Asian Crab Salad on Taro Chip
Camembert & Stone Fruity Chutney on Crostini

SALAD
Romaine & Mixed Greens with Cranberries, Chevre,
Candied Walnuts & Champagne Vinaigrette

ENTRÉE
Sea Bass with Smoked Tomato Vinaigrette, Herbed Risotto,
Winter Squash, Golden Beets & Yams
— or —
Beef Tenderloin with Mushroom Demi, Herbed Risotto,
Winter Squash, Golden Beets & Yams

DESSERT
Birthday Cake
Chocolate Cake with Raspberry Filling

Pan Seared Sea Bass with Tomato Caper Vinaigrette

3 ounces minced shallots

½ cup white wine vinegar

1 tablespoon Dijon mustard

1 tablespoon honey

½ lemon squeezed

1/2 cup capers

½ cup diced tomatoes

Russell's Original Seasoning,

to taste

2 cups olive oil

4–6 ounce sea bass portions

2 tablespoons olive oil

Russell's Original

Seasoning, to taste

VINAIGRETTE

In a small bowl, combine minced shallots, white wine vinegar, Dijon mustard, honey, lemon, capers, and tomato. Lightly whisk and then drizzle the olive oil while whisking. Refrigerate until the fish is cooked and ready to serve.

SEA BASS

Preheat oven to 450 degrees. Dry off the fish with a paper towel and season both sides. Heat a sauté pan on high heat, add olive oil and sear the sea bass flesh side down until golden brown. Do not flip the fish over. Put the sea bass into the oven for ten minutes. Fish should be cooked through.

Serve fish golden side up with a generous spoonful of the tomato caper vinaigrette over the top.

Fly Fishing: A Preface

Let's go fishing. It's the Fourth of July weekend on the Skagit River in Washington State. I'm under the influence of *Duende* and want to see if I might trick a steelhead. I have the latest sage rod and reel and an extra special pattern. I've procured a cabin up on Baker Lake. Everything is solid for making memories. I have my favorite hat, fishing shirt, and all weekend! I piece together my rod, and string it, tie on a sculpin pattern called a zoo cougar. In all the excitement, I forget to pinch the barb down. Pull out a desired amount of line to work with and, my friend, the wind plays the back-cast right on top of me. I try to roll-cast all this line forward and the hook finds a new home—right in my chest! Really sunk it home.

Gingerly, I tried to pull it out, but no chance, the barb was there to stay (99 percent of the time I pinch my barbs down for easier catch and release). I figured I could drink a bottle of pinot and take it out after daylight. So I fished all day and my new attachment lay in me until reality set in—bottle drained and still wouldn't pull out. Emergency room visit. No fish for the day, but even so, surely one of my best days on the river…

I have lived on the open ocean most of my life. Reading water is a skill set, whether surfing or standing in a river.

I started fly-fishing about fifteen years ago. It became a refuge. It is quiet and it is a way of reconnecting with nature. You can fly cast on rivers, lakes, and even the salt. The flora and fauna and the rich sea life constantly call you back to hone your skills. It is a great feeling knowing you are able to capture fish through natural patterns to outsmart them. Again, it forces one to ask, What does the fish see? What shades of colors? What patterns? Will it attack just anything or is it picky? Big fish don't get big eating nearly invisible bugs. Which shade of grey (out of the fifty) will create that predator/prey moment when the predator turns into a ballistic missile and your fly is the chosen!

As to the process: determine the kind of fish you are after and then, ask, what does said fish eat? Better yet, get the fish into "anger mode" by setting a fly next to their redd (the redd is a nest where the female has swept her tail on the gravel bar, making a space to lay her eggs; the male comes up behind her to fertilize the eggs); any threat near the redd threatens them and makes them go crazy. I want the fish to strike the fly, not just get snagged somewhere on the body. The simple version: Wrap thread around the shank of the hook, set a surface to cling to and start attaching various feathers and fur to resemble a baitfish or insect. Sounds easy. It's not! When you tie your own flies, you have to think of what

the fish might be eating and why—and tie your fly accordingly. Big fish search for proteins. How much energy will it take to capture and eat that meal? Color attracts predatory fish. They see it and attack out of hunger or anger. It is a great feeling knowing you are able to capture the fish through his own patterns of hunger and predation, to outsmart him. Again, it forces you to ask, *what does the fish see? What shades of colors? What patterns?*

Fly-fishing is wonderfully relaxing (when you don't hook yourself). Tying your own fly takes practice, materials and know-how, plus patience, and some ingenuity (if I may say so). Some tying experiments don't work. Then a few do work and you have to figure out why. Sometimes fish go for the bigger ones, sometimes for the more artistic ones.

Most of the time, fishing is catch and release. What is the fun in catching the fish and not keeping it? Well, it is the pure pleasure of interaction and attraction; gaining the total attention of the fish, getting the fish to react, the violent reaction, followed by the beauty of the run, finally the struggle. You test your talent with the fly, you think like the fish—the perfect relationship.

Pan-Fried Trout

4 whole rainbow trout,

1 pound each

3 garlic cloves, minced

1 pound chopped bacon,

reserve bacon fat

4 fresh basil leaves, chopped

1 teaspoon fresh thyme

1 lemon

2 tablespoons fresh chopped parsley

2 tablespoons of flour

Russell's Original Seasoning

Preheat oven to 350 degrees. First, de-bone fish. Start at the end fin and split on either side to tail. Use a serrated knife for this part. Then, separate the backbone down the length on either side from the collar to the tail. Detach the head and collar and the tail leaving only the two flesh sides of the fish. Spread the two sides of fish open to expose the rib bones. Use a filet knife to lift off the rib bones in 3 to 4 bone sections. After those bones are removed, remove the pin bones by cutting along either side in a V shape.

In a sauté pan large enough for your trout, crisp chopped bacon and remove from pan, leaving the bacon fat.

Once the fish is fileted, open it up flesh exposed. Season fish and rub with fresh garlic & herbs. Lightly dust in flour. Sauté in bacon fat, flesh side down for approximately three to four minutes until golden brown. Turn fish once and cook for additional two to three minutes. Squeeze ½ lemon on each fish and top with crispy bacon and chopped parsley. Serve now.

Fly Fishing in Baja

The following is a fly-fishing adventure, told from my journal entries on a recent trip to a secret locale in Baja. I went with fly fishermen extraordinaires, Bruce McNae and Kurt Beardslee.

DAY ONE

Departed the McNae Ranch with Kurt Beardslee. Bruce's wife Jean taxied us to SeaTac airport. Declined pay for meal on flight. Garbage in hotbox—not a good thought. Stunning country all the way to San Diego. Would love to explore back country along flight path. Yosemite looked awesome. Hope to shake stress soon. Looking down at the dry arroyos, I thought of Grandad Beattie. He would know how to get at the gold that washes through them. The old miner. Wish I could tie flies on trip...had to stow my box and tools in baggage.

Second leg: left San Diego, flying down peninsula. Would love to roam wild areas, super dry, lots of awesome surf in view. Unreal canyons and dry riverbeds. Must be lots of dry sluice opportunities. Immigration forms are a pain in the ass.

Arrived in Los Cabos, crazy x-ray, landing, tarmac, and screening. Red tarp rental, one-hour drive, dangerous highway, Buena Vista, way cool bougainvilleas and hibiscus. Palm trees, sleepy fishing villages. Rolling brown hills with desert-like scrub, like some parts of Eastern Washington. But always within view, the gorgeous blue water of the Sea of Cortez.

At the hotel beautiful pools, swim up bar, nobody here. Fished this evening. Caught eye of one big moray, followed my fly, I'm very happy with my flies. Walked a long way with Bruce McNae, three miles or so. We met up with Kurt Beardslee who was spey rod casting—can't wait to try that.

Kurt has great rhythm with his spey rod. He is not usually interested in the mullet method (bait and switch?); he likes sight casting. He tracks a table of coral, slinging flies wide from a spey rod, stripping it, moving legs in sync with the waves, and rocking of the boat. It is a thing to behold. There is so much energy in the rod...like a reverse punch in karate where you discover core energy and so much power…Karate Master Shihan Minakami would be proud…there is a whole art to it…and Kurt has it down.

Dinner with Bruce and guests—cats, about a half dozen of them, milling around at dinner time. McNae really attracts them. Swear he's got some mysterious kind of Doctor Doolittle thing going on. Animals, all animals, wild, tame whatever, just love him. He's sitting in a chair one minute; you look away, and then look back at him, and he's got a cat or a puppy (or both) in his lap. He talks to them, too.

After dinner, we tied leaders. A shower and now lights out to beat the snore forthcoming! Have a panga for tomorrow.

DAY 2

Breakfast and to the boat. Kurt and Bruce take off and leave me to my own panga. The panga, by the way, is the official (or unofficial) boat of Baja: it is a low, sturdy craft from 15 to 25 feet long, with a covered wheel hatch in the middle and an outboard motor. It has a low and open feel. It is ideal for fly-casting; roomy enough for two fishermen and a captain.

My captain's name is Enrique; he's a family man with three kids and has been running pangas for twenty years. I bet he knows every nook and cove, every shallow and reef. I bet he knows moods and seasons of the weather along with the fish temperament and the changes in the fish patterns (schooling).

You learn, in short order, that you don't need to go too far from shore, as the water gets deep very fast. With such depth comes an incredible variety of sea life. The panga lets you see the amazing proliferation of life around the beaches, where you have shallow reefs that go on for miles. Incredibly rich and diverse marine life, constantly generating the cycle of life.

For bait, live mullet. Wow. So the captain lets out a mullet, sixteen inches in length, it's hooked in lip and slowly trolled out about 25 feet behind the panga. When mullet starts swimming erratic we know it's scared. The boat captain shouts, "¡Está Caliente! ¡Está caliente!" Things are hot, it's time to play! The rooster comes shooting in after the mullet. When his dorsal fin springs up, he's determined and violence is in the air.

I threw a fly pattern right beside it and started stripping. The captain reels in the mullet. In the turmoil, the angry rooster hit my fly hard and took off. Forty-five minutes later with no camera (!) and no pals around, except the captain, we released a beauty, a thirty-pound rooster. No camera, bummer. What a fight and what colors. Using a nine weight RL Winston and Tibor reel, with intermediate line. Perfect combo.

Think of the everyday sayings, "bait and switch," "get your hackles up." Well, I'm living those expressions. You've got one bait rod and you've hooked on a live baitfish; you pick the baitfish out of the bait well on the boat, hook it through the lip and toss it out on your fixed line. It gets the attention of a bigger fish…you see your bait fish panic…it knows it's going to get eaten…the roosterfish go after it, you can see their hackles rise…you don't want the roosterfish to eat the live mullet. That is when you bait and switch. You start reeling in as fast as you can so he can't catch the mullet and then you cast  your fly. The roosterfish is mad and suddenly the fly appears—the mullet has been switched out.

Why do they choose my fly? I see the pink in the mullet and I tie it into my fly; I tie in lots of pink bucktail.

Wow, saw large whale breach and followed the coastline for many miles.

DAY 3

What a day today! We were ready. Tied flies the night before. I tied two super blue ones. Bruce and Kurt tied some real winners too. First thing, we could not find any mullet so the bait had us waiting. As soon as we got some bait, well, game on. I caught another rooster on the fly I tied. What a fight, it almost spooled me (that is, almost took all the line off my reel).

Baja is so full of giant predatory fish. They circulate in the reefs and when they see that mullet, all hell breaks loose. It is explosive. The surface becomes a stage of tremendous agitation. At first, the water swells then it stirs and seems to sizzle. You witness the extreme wild hunger of these fish, the quest for protein that is the life of the ocean. Sometimes you'll see six or seven roosterfish tracking the live mullet bait. They'll move into a circle like a roundup. Mullets travel in schools and roosterfish will go into a feeding frenzy, swallowing whole as many as their mouths can take in. Again, that boiling seizure erupts. Roosterfish can get up to one hundred pounds; they are giants. The bigger they get the harder it is to catch them on the fly. You can't trick them with bait and switch. A big rooster will get the bait before you can reel it in. And they must get smarter as they grow; I've never heard of anyone catching a large, say eighty to one hundred pound roosterfish on a fly. Even if you could, how would you handle such a violent, writhing fish after you hook it on your fly rod?

Anyway, I caught one, a good size, at least thirty pounds. We took some fine photos and released him. Then I caught a jack crevale and a superb ladyfish (like a miniature tarpon). Wow, did they fight! Hit hard! And—you guessed it—on the same fly. Saw a big rooster maybe fifty pounds. Then hooked into another rooster, same fly, but this time he broke off the fly. Four fish, one fly, not bad. And the day was not over! Wind came up and we slowly made our way back. That's when, alongside our panga, a three to four hundred pound black marlin swam, not a hundred yards from the shore. I took some photos as best as I could with the wind making waves and causing us to bob up and down. He was in twenty feet of water just under the surface, wow! This just doesn't happen. There's my Duende! I told myself. The captain said he had only seen this one other time in his life. Very rare.

We came in and shared photos and somehow I broke my rod. Major sadness! Played some pool and had a Mexican dinner. Tied some more winners tonight. Kurt and I tried brother Ron's spey rod on the beach this evening. Looks like I'll be benched tomorrow until I learn to use this new rod. The spey rod usually requires two hands to cast it. If you learn the technique, learn to roll and direct your cast, you can get tremendous power behind it. So it's a spey for tomorrow and a long walk. Kurt went to try new fly! Having a blast!

DAY 4

First light, breakfast of Spanish omelets with fresh papaya and watermelon and tremendous sunrise. In attendance—Bruce, Kurt and myself.

Today I became a fan of the spey rod. What an awesome outing, walking the beach. I got set up and within five casts, I was putting the line out a considerable distance—at least the thirty-inch needlefish thought so. I had to forfeit one of my favorite flies. I released him healthy, minus the unnatural fly hanging from his jaw. I wonder what happens to him now, swimming around, attracting other fish who might think he is biting into a meal. Will he become the meal?

Met Fred from Anaconda, Montana this morning. May go out with him later; he has a nice boat and knows how to fish with the fly! Would like to catch a Mahi on the fly. The rooster is tough to catch on the fly.

The wind came up hard now and it is hot today. I'm staying on shore. I don't want a fly in the chest in Mexico (see preface). Bruce and Kurt out on water today. Hope they win that rooster today.

Two Dorado and two skipjack, no roosters. Were not on it until the end of day. Two monsters at thirty pounds attacked the mullet and we couldn't turn them. Time to tie some flies. Met Bruce and Kurt coming in from fishing. Nada.

Mobile dock, put in and out daily, becomes a reef, and baitfish hide from the big roosters. What a display of roosters attacking baitfish!

Cast from beach tonight. A big fish grabbed latest fly and snapped the leader due to my error. Fish won! Think it was a big rooster.

No billiards for me tonight, Bruce and Kurt are pretty good though. I'm not that great (nice way of saying I suck). Dinner—Greek salad, tortilla soup and pork medallions with caramelized onion and mashed potatoes. Very good. Met some old codgers and traded hooks and flies (and fibs). Then tied more flies. Will

have a boat ready to go in the morning. Same captain. We are going to nail it tomorrow. Went for midnight swim not thinking about Humbolt squid, hammerhead sharks, or tiger sharks.

DAY 5

I'm a spectator. Beached. Today I didn't go out on the panga. I hit the beach with my spey rod just walking along throwing it out a long way. The line actually sings a note as you let it fly. You can catch amazing things, not always wanted like needlefish with that long sharp snout. How do you get your fly out of a mouth like that? If you hook one you just cut it loose. Or how about eels with their mouths full of sharp teeth? How are you going to catch and release those little monsters? The ladyfish are explosive when they hit. You catch them on little flies too. They are hard on the rods. You are moving constantly, the sand is hot. Hard to walk. Got to make sure you don't get burned. Wear a big hat, cover your feet, arms and legs—and this is May. The hotter it gets, the more fish school—tuna and marlin, searching for the baitfish schools. Not a place you want to take lightly. I went swimming. Take a few chances. You don't always know what is in the water.

The variety of the species is vast…you don't know what you're going to catch…

you try a small fly…eel go crazy for flies…Bruce and Kurt are incredible fishermen, so many years, they talk about knots, debate theories—whether a fly tracks upside down or right side up. The fly you tie doesn't mean it's going to track well. I like to try them out at Lake Washington, strip it in just to see how it's swimming…

The guys dropped me off on a desolate beach where I caught ten ladyfish on small tube flies. Awesome fight, would love my six-weight rod for this—walked down to a point. Beautiful right-hander peeling down the beach. Tried to take photos, wish I had my old Cannon A1.

Then we rendezvous and we're now back in the panga. I'm watching the legends work the magic. Kurt sure can cast.

This evening no catch, playing pool, one beer. I could live here. Tie flies and fish.

Primarily an older crowd. Hot weather coming soon. June is tuna but very hot wind. Would love to come in March for yellowtail (hot action, ¡Está Caliente!). Kurt just drew the pool cue without a tip. Usually reserved for me. I did not beat him one game. No problem, I am horrible at pool.

Back to my beach walk. This morning the wind was off shore and the water perfect. I had to stop and give thanks: this does not get better. Ladyfish offshore, follow turquoise water and nobody around—nobody—three hours later the "viejos" picked me up and I captained the boat and had to take a rooster on bait. I don't feel bad about it. I was working and we had a great release. The jetty was popping. I don't think I might witness two guys again as good as these guys. Double take, two ladyfish and unreal jumps. Fantastic fellowship. Found out Kurt likes Brown Water (Scotch).

There are trophy fish surrounding us here in the little bar. Stunning is the word. Can't stop admiring them. I will post the photos and trophy of my rooster at Russell's. Did I say, hard to catch on the fly! Going to go down to salt for swim. Can't get enough! My shoulders ache from casting and I still want in. I hear July is good here, may try to return. Really could live here…

Marlin for dinner and Mahi ceviche. Black Marlin was general consensus on what we saw; very rare sighting. No flies tonight (dumbbell heads for Coho salmon). Can't wait to get some salmon on the fly. Walked barefoot in sand this afternoon and burned the hell out of my feet. Swim this afternoon. Had a Cuba Libre. Was tasty.

Pan Seared Roosterfish with Red Pepper & Papaya Salsa

1 red pepper, roasted and diced

1 yellow pepper, roasted and diced

1 papaya, diced

½ red onion, minced

2 cloves garlic, minced

2 tablespoons fresh lime juice

½ bunch cilantro, minced

3 tablespoons olive oil

1 tablespoon raspberry vinegar

or apple cider vinegar

2 teaspoons kosher salt or season to

taste with Russell's Original Seasoning

4 - 6 ounce portions

of roosterfish

2 tablespoons of olive oil

Russell's Original Seasoning

RED PEPPER & PAPAYA SALSA

Prepare ingredients as directed, combine all, and toss well. Allow salsa to marinate in the chiller for at least one hour, up to one day. Toss again and add seasoning to taste before serving.

ROOSTERFISH

Pat dry each portion of fish, then season liberally on both sides. Preheat oven to 400 degrees. Heat an oven safe sauté pan and add two tablespoons of oil. Once the pan is hot, add the fish, flesh side down into the oil. Sear the fish until it turns golden brown on the one side. Do not flip the fish over or try to move it around. Place the whole pan in the oven for five to seven minutes, or until the fish is cooked through. Please do not overcook this fish.

Serve golden side up.

The Bear Hunt

Note: This is a chapter about hunting. Please skip over this chapter if details of predator and prey make you uncomfortable. For me there is a distinct connection between being a chef, that is, preparing animal proteins for my guests, and hunting. It is intimate beyond words. There is the heft of a weapon and the efficiency of a knife. I see both as a confrontation with myself and a test of my courage facing the act—the two are intertwined except that I am a participant in the one.

There is a special time of year, spring; a special place, Montana—and a special guide service that will take you bear hunting. You arrive in Montana, the northwestern quadrant, one hundred square miles of wide, rough mountain terrain near Glacier National Park. There is still a lot of snow. That's okay because it gives you something to track the bears in. Two seasons allow for bear: the spring hunt and the fall hunt. If you're unsuccessful in the spring you've still got the fall.

I am joined by four other hunters. There is a rustic but comfortable lodge with individual cabins and a respectful sense of camaraderie. But we also eye each other, try to test one another, try to smoke each other out. *Is he for real? Can he make it? Is he going to fold when the going gets rough? Is he a serious hunter? Who will be the one to get a bear?* We're heading into a hundred square miles of wilderness; nobody is opting for horse travel, the snowline is too low, and it's still too deep to allow the horses to go far. The hiking will be rigorous. Conversation reveals that everyone on the trip is an experienced hunter; maybe they have killed fifteen or twenty bears among them. They were definitely experienced hunters.

What will qualify me as a good hunter? It is more than just having good quality, sighted in guns. You must know how to walk, how to read the wind, how to be quiet. It is easy to pull the trigger. But what happens next? (Every year in some state, someone ends up on the wrong end of the scope. You can't call back a bullet.) We are not party hunting—we're going out individually—so you want to know the hunters who will be in the vicinity. Safety prods you to get to know your fellow hunters. You look at their boots, their bows, binoculars, the make and model of their guns and listen to their stories. Did the bow hunter bring a target?

(Serious bow hunters usually do.) You want to make sure your bow is not off or jarred. Same with your rifle. The guides want to know your accuracy and grouping. Everything has a purpose and is ready. What makes a good hunter? Know who you are and how you are going to respond to a given situation.

Each state has its own special rules for bear hunting. The state of Montana and a few other states have a black bear and grizzly bear identification test. You must take it before you can buy a bear license. You go online and you will see various scenarios of grizzly and black bears. (Hint: For starters, grizzlies have short rounded ears, a slightly indented face, and a hump at the neck with haunches shorter than their forelegs. Both grizzlies and blacks change colors during the seasons.) Grizzly or black—you have to be able to distinguish in the heat of the moment. The thing is, you don't always have time to tell which is which. You can't spot a bear and say to yourself, Ah, let's wait and see (as he runs into the bushes where you won't see him again). Grizzly or black? You really need to be careful. If you accidentally shoot a grizzly—or a momma bear with cubs—there is a monetary fine, a jail term, or both.

Back at the lodge, you always put your paw out on the table. The other hunters are going to share something and I want to share something in return. Each brought his drink of choice, some wine, but mostly scotch—McCallan, Laphroaig, Balvenie—and they set the bottles up on the table. Usually, during hunting season, I barely touch alcohol. You have all year to enjoy wine or whatever but during the season, it makes you gray and you need that added edge of sobriety. But I'm a good sport. I put a couple bottles of Château Margaux up on the table and said, "Gentlemen, I'm not going to touch these until I have some success. These are not to be opened until you see the paw of the bear." They looked at me and nodded. They didn't know me but I could tell they were probably thinking, *well, here's an Alcoholics Anonymous guy, at least he knows his wines.* That was fine with me. The whole idea in any hunting situation is that you cannot be gray—especially on a bear hunt. Even though you think you deserve that drink—you've had a hard hike that day or it's just been a long day—whatever. Tomorrow, when you need to make a split-second decision and you make the wrong choice, then what? What are you going to blame it on, alcohol?

Our guide is Jack. He's confident, in good shape, wilderness-ready, a survivor, crack shot, careful in gesture and speech, conversant with the territory and a good group psychologist to boot. He knows how to keep competitive men on an even keel. He knows men, bears, packhorses, dogs, and the endurance qualities of each. He has studied the habits of bears and can spot where they have swiped their claws on the bark of a hemlock trunk or when they have last sampled the skunk cabbage.

My first day out I did manage to see a grizzly, or run into one. He was a beautiful chocolate-gold bear, sniffing the air while standing in the brush. The afternoon light heightened his color and disarmed me. I should have been afraid but I wasn't. I was so taken with the majesty of the animal, it didn't matter that I was carrying firepower. You don't shoot grizzlies. If he came after me, where was I going to go? There were no climbable trees around. So far, he hadn't detected me. I stood still and the fear hit me as I watched him sniff, turn, and take me in his sight. He had gotten wind of me and he looked right at me. Then he ran away. Grizzlies are an apex predator, you are the visitor and if they see you, sometimes they will come and check you out. I breathed out and walked back to the trailhead.

I've been in a few other situations with bears where I really had to think about my departure. How do I get out of the situation? During hunts where I have slept in trees, I've heard bears down below me sniffing around scratching around. I had to think, *should I light them up or not?* No, I can't just shoot in the dark and hit a grizzly bear. If you put a headlamp on him, he may or may not move. He might just ask himself, *what is that? I'd better have a bite!* Bears are unpredictable animals. Nine out of ten times luck might be on your side, but on that tenth time—he's eating you! You just don't know.

I have had my gun scope up on a bear, studying him, making sure; he turns out to be a grizzly *(way to go Russ)*. You are so excited—your adrenaline is up all the way. Your heart is trying to kick its way out of your chest. You can barely maintain calm. If your guide is with you—his head will be practically next to yours—you whisper, is this the right bear? Is this a good-looking specimen? (Dialogue ensues: Yes? No? Yes? Maybe?) His time in the field should help you to determine, *yes this is a black bear, this a good bear to shoot.* The guide is looking for the cubs or he's scanning for the marks of a grizzly bear, the hump in the back, the dishpan face. If the guide is with you and he tells you: *give him the pepper* he had better be right.

You're paying him to get it right.

On another spring bear hunt in Montana, I was accompanied by two friends, first timers on a hunting trip. I had asked them to come along to help me pack out

my (hoped for) success. We were taking a break from walking a ridgeline and I was looking across at a north slope where bears come out of hibernation. I began howling like an injured animal. *Awwwooo! Wah wha!* Let them come: cougar, coyote, wolf—first one there gets free meal.

It was a stunning afternoon in Montana, blue sky, the open spread of wilderness surrounding us, majestic trees in all shades of green against the snow line. I just had to shout: *Look where we are!* My companions looked at me. I could tell they were getting a bit nervous; neither of them had much experience in the wild. I knew they had never seen a bear in the wild. Again I cried out like a wounded ungulate, howling over the ridgeline into the

drainage below. I took my binoculars and began glassing down the slopes, studying the open areas and fingers between the buck brush and maples. The trail is steep and the scree is slippery. Suddenly I see the hindquarter of a large chocolate-phase bear. My predator calling worked too well. The bear emerges in full: it's a grizzly. We have to move, we have to vacate our comfortable but tick-infested, rock outcropping chairs. Hurriedly I looked through the binoculars. I confirmed that we have sighted a radio-collared grizzly bear.

He looks around and vaguely starts towards us. My friends see him too, and worse, he sees us. He must be all primed for a big meal. We packed up fast. We were standing on a ridgeback trail so narrow that only a goat could feel safe on it.

We took off running and made a circle. We either lost the bear or tired him out. We ended up at the head of a big basin. It bothered me that I had almost shot it, a grizzly. My friends were yelling and scared, *Why did we come on this hunt? Russell is crazy. Russell, you're crazy.* I tried to calm them, *hey guys, we got to the basin safely.* To myself I thought, *that was close.*

Later I talked to a friend who knows the drainage. I said, "Let's report the grizzly with the collar." We called the biologist.

We'd like to report a radio-collared grizzly sighting.

"That's impossible," the biologist said. "I have radio-collared every grizzly in Montana and I've never seen one in that area." Later the biologist called the owner of the property to get a profile on me. (To check me out!) Turns out, the bear was radio-collared in Canada. He had ranged over hundreds of miles. A year later, at the same camp, I saw a huge placard:

Grizzly bear country.
Know your bear!
(Shows the two different kinds of bear)

On another occasion, I was hunting with my brother. We sat down and took out our peanut butter and jelly sandwiches. We couldn't believe it—a bear is ambling towards us on the ridge trail. By the time I knocked an arrow, the bear was practically upon us. He was too close for me to release the arrow. I waved an arm and roared as if I were a bear. He stood up waving his paws and sniffing the air, trying to make out what I was. Bear eyesight is not so good but I think my camo helped hide me too. My arrow was at the ready but, again, he was too close and now the underbrush was covering his vitals. Without thinking, I squeaked out, "Kitty kitty." I wanted him to move slightly and give me a shot. With incredible speed, the bear dove over the steep and into the thick—he just disappeared. After we calmed down and made sure the bear was really gone, my brother turned to me and said, "Did I just hear you say "Kitty kitty" to a bear?"

I think I should put in another plug for the bear test. Take the test; it's online— Montana, Fish, Wildlife & Parks. They present colorful pictures. In one shot the bear's head is in the bushes and you can't easily tell what kind it is. The authorities want you to be extra cautious during your hunt so that you don't kill that grizzly. The test wants you to hone your visuals. Things can go awry fast in bear encounters. You have to balance the thrill of the hunt with the obvious: bear hunting can be a dangerous pursuit; you can get killed or at best badly mauled.

I have to say again, when you see a bear, your adrenaline is on high—total *Go Power*. I have always taken care not to enter into bear hunting lightly. I've tried to make sure that my skill sets are honed. Nobody just picks it up one day and says, *I'm going bear hunting*. I think everyone at some point thinks of bears as cuddly little Smokey the Bear things. In reality, bears eat bears. Bears are not generally your furry friends. A grizzly bear doesn't look at a black bear and say, "Hi Cuz." He looks at a black bear and says, *dinner!* A grizzly bear will eat a black bear, right now, along with anything else (including you). A grizzly is not to be messed with.

Back to our hunting party, it's day four with no action and everyone is getting a bit restless. In civilian life, I've learned, they are doctors and lawyers, competitive men, guys who look for results. They've put in the hours and the hikes; they are genuine outdoor guys. You could drop them from a helicopter in the middle of the Rockies with a penknife and they would probably wander into the nearest town a day or two later, happy and healthy.

We all relax at dinner and start talking to each other. They find out I'm a chef. Conversation always comes back to bear. The men are starting to look at the guide who is taking our money and, to his credit, wanting us to get a kill. But, the unspoken thought goes around: *We came to hunt bear and none of us have even taken a shot at one (in an area supposedly crawling with bear!)* Then, the thoughts get spoken:

There's nothing out here.
They're still in hibernation.
I know there's a den nearby.
I saw some tracks.
Where were you?
We were up in the drainage.

I have a feeling that the spring bears are out. They just haven't meandered into their time-honored spots.

The guide can't control the weather; all he can do is put you onto something. We were lucky. Our early spring days were clear and gorgeous, letting us see many hundreds of yards without binoculars. It was early enough for dandelions and light greens—bears favorite food as they come out of hibernation (their stomachs are still fragile). When you start to see more and more dandelions, you know the bears are going to smell them and be on their way. This is what they're searching for.

By day five, our last day, the bottles of Château Margaux that I set out at the beginning are still unopened. My fellow hunters haven't said anything but their glances say, *aren't you going to open them?* "No," I say aloud to myself. "I really don't want to open them until I bring back a kill." They smile and nod and everyone sets out.

In the late afternoon, I finally spotted a black bear. He seemed like medium build, definitely not as big as the grizzly I saw on my first day. He was partly hidden by some brush and lifting his head sniffing out the afternoon. He wasn't going anywhere.

"Break that bear down so he can't run; take out his shoulder," the guide said.

He wasn't that big but when his hide is glistening, long hair fur standing up, he looks bigger than he might be. The guide said *go for it*. I'm serious, I don't want to kill unless he's a good bear. The guide knew I could shoot so I followed his lead. I settled into a stump, relaxed, and took aim. From about one hundred feet away I fired and got him in the shoulder. He didn't go down but wheeled around in circles like a dog with his tail pinched in a car door and then ran down a brush-choked ravine. He should have been dead but the adrenaline must have hit him and he took off.

The sun was setting and the direct light was disappearing fast. The guide didn't want to follow me down the ravine. He wanted to head back to camp and come looking for the bear in the morning. I didn't want to leave him all night, suffering with a nasty wound in one of his main extremities. The merciful thing to do would be to take responsibility, go down there and finish him off. Not leave him to suffer. That might sound callous but that would be the right thing to do.

I followed him down the ravine. It was really getting dark now. The trees were blending into the dark and taking on scary outlines. I was alone now and recalling that the guide didn't even offer to go down with me. The ravine was steep and I was forced to step down sideways to be careful of my ankles.

At the bottom lay a huge first-growth hemlock. It had a tremendous girth, so I was able to walk right on it as a bridge through the choked underbrush. Nearby, I spotted a stack of smaller fallen logs whose cross pattern formed a kind of nest. I took my time and walked along slowly, a careful step at a time. I knew the bear was taking refuge somewhere to the side of the giant trunk I was on. Wounded or no, he could jump out anywhere and maul you good. I walked on the old tree slowly, stopping and listening. I didn't hear anything.

After about twenty steps, the wounded bear jumped up from the nest of fallen logs and started for me. I hit him at close quarters three times in the chest with a .44 Smith and Wesson. He practically fell at my feet. The adrenaline rush was very real.

The guide heard the shots, came down, and gutted the bear. I carried the carcass out on my back.

"You must be an elk hunter," the guide said.

In retrospect, I wish I could have made a one shot, one kill with the bear.

Pulling into camp, the dogs picked up the bear scent. I've got bear blood all over my back. We had arrived before any of the other hunters and the dogs probably thought a bear was coming into camp. I took the tenderloins from the bear directly to the kitchen and sliced, seasoned, and sautéed them in a pan. I opened the bottles of Château Margaux to let the wine breathe.

Back at the lodge, the other hunters had settled in. Their boots were off and they had resigned themselves to a gameless hunt. Just as they observed the open bottles at the dinner table—*hey, did he get something?*—I came out serving the bear tenderloins.

It was a worthy finish to a great, intense trip.

Sautéed Bear Medallions with Roasted Shallot Butter Sauce

SERVES 4

20 ounces bear loin, sliced
into medallions ½" thick

3 medium size shallots,
peeled and sliced into rounds

Russell's Original Seasoning

3 tablespoons olive oil

2 ounces beef stock

2 ounces unsalted butter

Slice the bear loin on a bias into rounds. Season the bear meat liberally with Russell's Original Seasoning on both sides. Heat oil in a pan and gently lay the bear in a clockwise pattern into the hot oil. As you lay the last medallion in the pan, check the first piece of meat to see if it is ready to turn over. The meat will brown quickly. Monitor it closely and don't walk away. Cook each piece until lightly browned, approximately five minutes. Add shallots, beef stock, and unsalted butter. Serve now.

Road Kill in Malibu

I sometimes speak to business schools around our area. One of my main points I like to emphasize: *stay loyal to your friends. You never know what the future brings.*

I usually illustrate the point by bringing up my high school pal, Chris Chelios. We were close in high school, and soon after, Chris entered the minor leagues to play hockey in Canada. Before long, he was a top draft pick for the National Hockey League. He went on to have a successful career in the NHL, becoming a great national athlete. Just a few of his career highlights confirm this: member of three Stanley Cup winning teams, leading three U.S. Olympic teams (with a silver medal win in 2002), included on National Hockey League All-Star teams thirteen times and inducted into the Hockey Hall of Fame in 2013.

Chris and I have stayed in touch over the years; we try to support each other when we can. Chris' generosity and hospitality has allowed me and my family to share in his world while he has stayed a grounded, down-to-earth guy.

Chris has great energy—his professional career as a top hockey defenseman has given him a kind of physical command; it comes out in his posture. When he stands there in front of you, trying to persuade you of something, you can see why he was captain of the Chicago Blackhawks and later helped deliver the Detroit Red Wings the Stanley Cup in 2002 and 2008. *Persuasive* would be an understatement. At the same time Chris is very social, he enjoys people, he enjoys the life of a live hard, play hard athlete.

When Chris and I get together, something always seems to happen.

Try as I might to take it easy when we get together, *something always happens.* I try to steel myself against weird happenings, making resolutions beforehand—*we won't do this, or go there or do that*—it never seems to work.

Something always happens.

On this particular occasion, a friend of ours from high school had recently died. He was still young and we had been close in high school, growing up in the San Diego area. We ran together, surfed together, did all the things California teenagers do in the movies—driving around, hitting the beach, trying to meet girls, surfing, hanging out. Chris called me and said, "Come on down, it's a sad moment but we should be there."

This was right. We would pay respect to a friend from our youth and remind ourselves of the importance of friendship through life's ups and downs. It would be a somber, meditative occasion, a memorial service—what could go wrong? I was determined nothing would happen. I would go to the service and then come home. End of story.

Besides, I told Chris beforehand, I had to get back to work by the next Monday to cook for the King of Spain. Even if my client were my next-door neighbor, I would still want to be back on time and prepared mentally and physically to do a good job. It just happened that my client was the King of Spain. That wasn't the main point—I try to treat everyone like a king—but it did put a bit of edge on the occasion. If nothing else, he was a guest and you want him, like any guest, to walk away with a good impression.

I flew in to LAX and landed safely, always a relief. Then we (passengers) learned that the nose cone on the plane had broken and we couldn't taxi in. That was a bad omen. Meanwhile, Chris was driving around the airport while I sat in the plane waiting for them to fix the nose cone. Two hours later, we were able to taxi in to the gate. Chris picked me up and finally we were on the road heading to San Diego to meet up with high school friends who had gathered for the funeral. The weather was wonderful—typical California weather, sunny, nearly cloudless. The drive was great, but we were mostly quiet, in a funk, thinking about our departed friend.

In San Diego, we went to the funeral the next day. It was sad and we tried to find some meaning in it. Chris got up and spoke and gave a very moving address that I thought really comforted the family.

Afterwards, Chris and I were reflective, thinking of our friend and his life cut short. We wanted to do something or say something that would capture our friend's spirit in the way we remembered him when we were young. We didn't think the service hit the right tone. It was decently somber and respectful but something was missing. Our friend lived at the extremes and we knew that he wouldn't want us to feel so down.

Chris was restless. He said, "Let's do something, I don't know what."

"Okay." I hesitated, thinking about the King of Spain and my return flight.

I should have figured. Chris is world-famous for making all kinds of things happen. It is part of his job, out on the ice especially. He knows how to make things exciting for the fans and his fellow players (and opponents). When Chris wants to party, he can make it happen. He made a call to Nobu, a Malibu hot spot along the Pacific Coast Highway.

The restaurant is full? That's okay. Can we share a table? Sure, that will work.

We arrived at Nobu. The maître'd pulled out all the stops. We walked into the restaurant past a line thirty people deep. The waters part. Chris and I are ushered right in. This is Malibu. At the table sits Dustin Hoffman, Mark Wahlberg, Jeremy Piven and some of their friends looking like they're having a good time. Just another day in the life of Chris.

Part of what gets me into trouble is that I don't really follow Hollywood or sports figures and often I only have the vaguest idea of who anyone is. All through dinner, I kept needling Mark Wahlberg, telling him I could box and that I could spar with anybody. I didn't know he was in the middle of filming a boxing spectacular. Here I was challenging him to a match. *Another crazy fan*, Wahlberg must have thought. It was a testament to his good nature that Mark Wahlberg didn't take me seriously though at one point we did compare fists. We put them out on the table; his was twice the size of mine.

Back in Chris' car, we head home. We are driving down the Pacific Coast Highway and just as we get to Pepperdine University, we see a freshly hit mule deer in the middle of the road.

Arriving at Chris' I said, "Chris, we've got to go back for that deer." I was sorry to see it like that—it was flinching still and I wanted to go get it and put it out of its misery. Also, the chef in me is thinking *fresh protein*.

"What about the King of Spain?" Chris said. "If we go get this thing I'll need the chef around for a party."

I nodded. Chris called John Cusack. "We need your driving skills," Chris told him.

"Tell him to wear black," I said. This was going to be a night operation; I didn't want us to get caught.

John Cusack arrived with a friend and he got into the driver's seat of Chris' chop top Scout and we drove out to the highway. The deer was still there, though not moving now. Chris and I picked it up and threw it into the bed of the truck.

Once back at the house, I was able to look the poor thing over. We set it in the carport. Much of it was terribly bruised, indicating internal bleeding. I wasn't about to open it up.

"I'll just take the parts that aren't damaged," I said.

As I was standing over the deer, Chris came out with the knives.

"What are you going to do?" John Cusack asked.

"We're going to eat it," I said.

"Okay, bye," John said. He was off for filming in London the next day.

I cut off the hindquarters and back straps and left the forelegs on. The rest of the deer was unsalvageable. I felt myself taking on a chef's role: *use what is good, don't touch the damaged parts.* The carport looked like a slaughterhouse. We threw the rest into the ocean expecting the tide and sea life to take care of it.

Don't look in the icebox...

The next morning Chris' neighbor calls him early and says, "Chris! A great white shark bit a deer in half and he's washed up on our beach! You've got to help me tow it out offshore. I need to throw it back in the ocean. My grandkids are coming over and I don't want them to see this."

Chris and I got coffee and walked the stretch of beach over to his neighbor's property. We knew it was our deer carcass that had startled Chris' neighbor. We chuckled about it but figured it was more than possible for a shark to bite a deer in half in the ocean. Deer have been known to come down from the hills to the beach for the salt. About a half a mile out in front there was a shark pen—a place for fishermen to drop off sharks that they had inadvertently hooked. The pen had to attract all manner of ocean predators. In any case, by the time we arrived at the neighbors' the ocean—or something had carried the deer carcass off.

Meanwhile, we are back at Chris' house where the good parts of the deer are in the fridge. Then I hear Chris being Chris. He is on the phone, calling friends, organizing an impromptu party. "Russ," Chris says, "this is the right send-off for our pal. Fix that deer up, let's grill it and serve it to our guests."

"Okay." I said thinking about the King of Spain. I was starting to cut it close; I had to get back to Seattle.

That afternoon Chris threw a party. He invited friends to gather around in comfort and camaraderie. I took the hindquarters out of the fridge, prepped them, and cut generous medallions, grilled them and passed around trays when Chris' neighbors began to arrive in the afternoon.

"Have some road kill," I said while parking the serving dish before a guest.

Nervous laughter followed. Then exclamations: *Wow, this is great!*

Chris looked across the deck at me and raised a glass of wine. We had done right by our pal.

The next morning at a local breakfast hangout, on my way to the airport,

we were confronted by a famous actor. "Hey," the famous actor said, "I heard that you guys went and stole someone's pet deer and then carved it up and grilled it at a picnic." He was clearly upset with us.

No, no, we explained. That is not what happened. We told the famous actor our story but I don't know if he believed us. Stories travel and change in the travel, as everyone knows.

But this is what really happened.

(p.s. I got back in time, barely. By all accounts, the King of Spain was happy with his meal...)

Grilled Venison Brochettes

SERVES 8

Recommended cut of meat is the backstrap.

This is a very easy way to "wow" your guests at your dinner party. Soak the skewers in warm water for 30 minutes to prevent the wood from burning.

2 pounds cubed venison
1 red onion—1" cube
1 yellow bell pepper—1" cube
1 red bell pepper—1"cube

Cut the meat into chunks, roughly 1-by-1-inches

Cube all the vegetables and blanch in salted water for two to three minutes. Then skewer the meat and vegetables and season with Russell's Original Seasoning. Drizzle with olive oil and grill on high for three to five minutes. Baste with unsalted butter and serve now.

Maestro Schwarz

I wasn't raised around classical music. It was always a bit remote to me. But then I started doing dinners and a variety of events for Gerard Schwarz—conductor for the Seattle Symphony since 1985. I thought I'd better get with it and learn about this dynamic man.

Glancing at his resume, I learned that Gerard Schwarz is esteemed internationally as well as nationally, guest conducting all over the world. He was a force behind the building of Seattle's great concert hall, Benaroya Hall and an energetic fundraiser for the Seattle Symphony with whom he recorded over eighty CDs. He also founded the popular Mostly Mozart Festival and he was appointed to the National Council of the Arts Advisory Board in 2004 by President George W. Bush.

So, despite my ignorance of classical music, I thought I should probably treat Maestro Schwarz like other musicians I've known. Like chefs, musicians work late hours. They need a long tail to unwind and most of the time that means a good meal. Dinner for five after a concert night wouldn't be uncommon on the schedule.

"We're working men, Russell." I think those were the first words Gerard said to me when we first met. And it was true. You might have the greatest musicians in the world playing under your baton, but after work, *let's relax and eat*. Famous or not so famous, Gerard has a very direct way of making everyone feel special.

One time, at a Wild Fish Conservancy charity auction, Gerard offered a symphony night accompanying his wife Jody, followed by a meet-and-greet and dinner afterwards with the maestro and his wife. Somehow, I outbid everyone and won. (I'm still not sure how that happened since I had my eye on a Harry Lemire fly up for auction on that same occasion.) Anyway, the concert was Mozart's Requiem, and it was my first. Wow. The music was wonderful, overwhelming; it seemed to have weight; like standing under a musical waterfall. Such amazing musical power.

It was great being introduced to classical music by maestro Gerard Schwarz. My ignorance was (and still is) vast. To illustrate: one Saturday afternoon I was cutting meat by myself and listening to KING FM. A great piece of music came on that was quite drawn out and very beautiful. I think one movement lasted as long as it took me to go through a master case of tenderloin. I didn't catch the name of the piece (this was before the radio stations listed the playlists online). I only caught that it was a symphony by Gustav Mahler.

Next time I was on Queen Anne I stopped in at Tower Records and headed for the classical music department. The guys behind the counter in the classical section looked very serious and very knowing. You would have to be on your toes to approach them. I went to the counter and, in my best casual, but sophisticated, manner, said, "I'm looking for a symphony by Mahler."

"Okay," the bearded serious young man behind the counter said. "Which one? He wrote nine of them."

I said, "Well, it has a very long and stretched out movement in it."

The serious and knowing guys behind the classical counter burst out laughing.

"We've got news for you, pal," they said. "You've just described *all* of Mahler's symphonies."

My continuing adult education goes on.

Moving from music to food, I remember a Maestro's Circle event at the Schwarz's when over one hundred and fifty guests were waiting on dinner. For such a large group I had set up my 'Triage Kitchen' outside on the lawn under the trees. My Triage Kitchens are typically four ranges with ovens and burners along with serving tables and portable sinks. For some reason, none of the ranges would light. Try as we might the pilot lights kept going out; even when they lit, they wouldn't stay lit. We couldn't even cook the blinis. The vibe was good but I knew everyone was getting hungry. I needed to fire up the ovens but no dice.

I had to deliver the news to Gerard, point-blank. "I'm sorry but these ovens are not going to light." I said. "We need to buy some time." He gave me a confirming glance, nodded, and without missing a beat said, "Pizza! We'll order pizza. Don't worry about it."

Two feelings came over me at the same time. I admired Gerard's decisiveness. No blame, no drama, let's just try plan B. I imagined that, as an orchestra conductor, Gerard would have to move through problems of the moment with cool dispatch—a violinist breaks a string, a chair collapses, a cymbal drops or a music stand falls over. Keep going. On the other hand, my pride was seriously dented (as the Brits say); I had a great dinner planned and I just couldn't let pizza rule the day. Fortunately my lead waiter, a jack-of-all-trades, fashioned some working propane hoses. The pilot lights flared and stayed lit—the day was saved, dinner was served.

Gerard and Jody Schwarz are exceptional hosts and are frequently called upon to show visiting musical guests the special hospitality of the Pacific Northwest. They are great representatives of our area to the world. That is, when they host visitors from around the world, they really like to make them feel welcome; I always feel honored to help.

By the time famed cellist, Yo-Yo Ma, arrived to play with the Seattle Symphony, I had learned enough to know that he was a prodigy on the cello, that he had appeared on Johnny Carson at age ten and that as a young adult, he had impressed audiences worldwide with his playing. Yo-Yo Ma had also reached across musical genres to embrace jazz and pop and was credited, along with his musical accomplishments, with being a very nice man. This last trait I was able to test for myself.

I prepared dinner for fifteen that evening at the Schwarz's and Yo-Yo Ma arrived before anyone else. Always looking for his guests to feel welcome and connected, Gerard introduced me to Yo-Yo Ma as a fly fisherman. Gerard said, "He's our chef but he's also an expert fly fisherman."

We talked out on the deck and Yo-Yo Ma asked me questions

Russell with Gerard & Jody Schwarz

about fly-fishing. He expressed genuine interest and asked about where and how you fish on the fly. He said he would like to try it sometime. I felt very flattered that I could hold the interest of a world-famous musical star in this way and upon one of my favorite subjects. Then, I thought, Yo-Yo Ma must have to take in many of these dinners throughout the world. He knows how to be a good

guest. At the same time he did seem interested; I hoped he wasn't bored.

Even so, I really wanted to make sure. I couldn't resist the chance to test his reputation as a genuinely nice person...along with his newfound interest in fly-fishing. Was he just being polite? Hmmm. Let's see.

Back in the kitchen, I was doing prep for the dinner and supervising the serving staff. *Mise en place*, as they say. I remembered that in my truck, I had a few new fly-fishing flies. Meanwhile, dinner was going well. Every so often, I would peek out from the kitchen just to make sure the course timing was spot on. Then I went out to my truck and grabbed the newest edition to my fly box and pressed it into an empty tin of Altoids breath mints. Surreptitiously, I asked my head server to set the Altoids tin beside Yo-Yo Ma's wine glass.

Next time I looked out the kitchen door I paused and motioned Yo-Yo Ma to look down. He did and noticed the small tin of Altoids. He looked up at me and I pointed to my mouth. He nodded, believing that I was advising him on his breath. Dutifully he swept the can off the table and opened it on his lap.

Instead of a collection of white breath mints, he saw the small colorful fishing fly that I had set inside the tin. He looked up at me and gave that great beaming smile. Yes, here was a genuinely good-humored and nice man. We had a good laugh with Gerard, Jody, and everyone after dinner.

I'm still waiting (hoping) to take Yo-Yo Ma fly fishing on his next visit to Seattle.

Menu for Yo Yo Ma

PASSED HORS D'OEUVRES
Poached Chicken & Avocado Terrine on Walnut Crisp
Chive Crepe with American Sturgeon Caviar, Hard Cooked
Quail Egg, Shallots & Crème Fraîche
Riesling Poached Foie Gras Torchon with Fig Preserves
Ratatouille Barquette

STARTER COURSE
Smoked Guinea Fowl Salad with Hazelnuts & Granny Smith Apple

ENTRÉE
Filet of Beef with Caramelized Sweet Onions,
Butternut Squash Risotto & Demi Glace
— or —
Alaskan Halibut & Spot Prawns with Baby Zucchini &
Crookneck Squash, Fingerling Potatoes & Smoked Tomato
Infused Olive Oil

DESSERT
Rhubarb Financier with Strawberry Gelée
Chocolate Hazelnut Feuillitine Tuile, Lemon-Basil Syrup
& Caramel Sauce

Butternut Squash Risotto

SERVES 6

2 cups ½ inch by ½ inch

cubed squash

1 tablespoon fresh thyme

1 cup plus ¼ cup for garnish

shredded parmesan

1 tablespoon chopped parsley

for garnish

1 cup diced yellow onion

4-6 pints chicken stock

3 cups dry Arborio rice

Russell's Original Seasoning,

to taste

3 tablespoons butter

3 tablespoons olive oil

SQUASH

Preheat oven to 450 degrees. Peel, cut and roast squash with one tablespoon olive oil. Toss with seasoning on a sheet pan and roast until fork tender. Approximately ten to fifteen minutes. Set aside and cool.

RISOTTO

Heat chicken stock. In a separate saucepan sauté diced onion with two tablespoons olive oil for three minutes. Add Arborio rice and stir for another two minutes. Slowly add chicken stock allowing the rice to absorb the stock. Continually stirring, add more stock until rice is cooked through, approximately eighteen to twenty minutes. Fold in butter, one cup parmesan, squash, thyme and season to taste. Risotto should not hold its shape on a plate—if it does, add a small amount of stock to loosen up. Garnish with parmesan cheese and parsley.

Cuba (Slight Return)

Recently I had the good fortune to return to Cuba. I went as part of a cultural exchange and fly-fishing tour. We stayed in Havana for one night and headed out to the waters the next day. I can't really add much original to the descriptions of present day Havana. I saw what everyone sees: the beautiful and majestic city in desperate need of a face-lift, the wonderfully restored and maintained American cars from the 1940s and 50s. At the same time, I did have the privilege of mixing with some Cubans in their homes and the neighborhood; they were incredibly warm and hospitable. It was great fun to speak to them in Spanish.

One evening I met a friendly pedicab driver who asked me and one of my fly-fishing pals, John Hyde of the Yamsi Ranch in Oregon, "Do you want to go to a restaurant?" The pedicab is a bicycle-powered cab with a two-seat carriage attached. He was elderly, gray haired, of wiry build and, presumably, in great shape from wheeling his cab all over Havana. He was so friendly that I blurted out, "Let's go eat where you eat!" After about fifteen minutes of passing through side streets, pastel colored buildings, dark alleyways, and classic old structures, we came to a stop. We entered a pink building and walked up three flights of barely lit stairs. We were welcomed into a flat and the driver introduced us to a middle-aged woman with a gracious smile who sat us at her dining table. The TV was on showing a musical variety show. Children and grandchildren came in looking us over shyly.

Within minutes, the most wonderful smells gathered around us. Before long, the smells turned into the classic Cuban cuisine: black beans and rice, fried plantain and chicken cutlet. What a treat! Such a great meal and on such short notice. ¡Bien hecho!

I didn't get the impression that anyone was excited about politics or the current political situation but then I tried not to pry. I was a visitor and I wanted them to be happy I came. As I say, I wasn't there long and I can only offer a few impressions. The infrastructure seemed to have a worn and tired feel to it. Yes, great beauty and grandeur but still worn and tired—even the cows in the countryside seemed worn and tired.

Another thrill was going out every morning to new locations to explore the coves and inlets and reefs and reliving the memories of my youth. It was a different part of the island but still wonderful and very similar to what I remembered. The mangrove fingers and inlets were still there. We saw where hurricanes had torn across certain parts and left long swaths of dead vegetation. But right behind them was the new growth flourishing under the protection of the wasted patches as it only can in the tropics. Speaking of hurricanes, one afternoon we came upon a boat graveyard. There's nothing like seeing a shrimper hull big as a city bus cast upon the shore to impress upon you the power of nature in the tropics.

The water in the shallows was as gin-clear as I remembered it and all the schools swarmed back: bonefish, snapper, cowfish and puffer fish. You are three men to a small shallow outboard motor boat called a Dolphin: two fishermen and one Cuban guide who steers the boat through the shallows. One fisherman stands on the bow and casts, a skill in itself since it's not uncommon to flip into the water or capsize the craft. The other fisherman sits in the middle, waiting, watching, gathering line or tying leaders.

I was so happy to be able to confirm my childhood sense of exploration: the beautiful scenery, the shallows, the mangroves, the reefs and inlets. And the abundance of fish is not to be believed, almost like fishing in an aquarium. I was only surprised at the heat. The temperate marine climate of the Pacific Northwest does not prepare you for the tropics. You absolutely cannot go out without head covering or sunscreen or you will get burnt up. But everything else was as I remembered it. Unforgettable, the explosive feeling that you're drawing out of a tumultuous underwater life. The water seemed crammed with fish competing for flies. I was especially proud that all my flies attracted fish and all of them got gobbled in the maelstrom that is fishing the Cuban reefs.

Hunting the shallows one afternoon, I cast a fly into the surf just peeling over a reef. It landed perfectly, right in the trough and the take was amazing. The fish took off with tremendous flight and resistance. A beautiful tarpon, seventy or eighty pounds, he jumped ten times in twenty minutes. You felt these great waves or surges of competitive, predatory energy—life wanting to devour everything in sight. After about thirty minutes, I brought him to hand at the boat and gave him a nice clean release.

The next day saw a wonderful bright blue morning in the Caribbean and our group was eager to head out. There were eight of us and we rotated partners, two per boat plus our Cuban guide. The Cuban guides, by the way, are considered some of the best saltwater fishing guides in the world; a new guide doesn't usually appear unless an old one dies. Anyway, back in our boat the guide is perched up on the stern, standing and looking. The idea is that he can see where the fish are since his platform is the highest section of the boat. I sat in the middle of the boat tying leaders. My fishing partner for that day was Tom. He stood on the bow and cast.

The guide tried to direct our casts, yelling, in heavily accented English: "More right! *¡Mas a la derecha!* More right! *Ah, se fue,* he's gone." Of course, the fish is on the left by the time you cast. The guide yells, "More left! Left! *¡Mas a la izquierda!* Left!" On cue, the fish swerved right as soon as Tom cast left. The guide was getting even more frantic than the fish we were chasing. His tip depends upon a successful catch so he is pretty much yelling constantly. It's an understatement to say he has no bedside manner.

Tom is a good fishing partner. I peg him in his mid-sixties; he's still got his hair and rocky good looks and wears that rugged western confidence. He is an experienced fisherman and you can tell he's a guy not easily rattled. Between casts and through the hollering of our guide, we talk a bit distractedly, trying to get acquainted. He tells me a bit about himself in an offhand manner and I listen in an offhand manner...screenplays...books...movies...horses...writer...Movies? Yes...*The Missouri Breaks. Really? The Missouri Breaks?* Wow, one of my favorite movies. Tell me your name again? Tom McGuane...

I'm sitting in a shallow boat under a Caribbean sun, surrounded by marvels and it dawns on me that my boat mate is a man of spectacular accomplishments. So many cool things happening. Meanwhile, the guide continues to holler directions

at Tom who glances at me and gives me a look that says: *you take over for a bit this guy is getting on my nerves.*

Now I'm standing in the bow and the guide keeps up his yelling routine, "Right! More Right! *¡Izquierda!* More Left!" Indeed it is very distracting. He keeps yelling, "More left! More left!" The fish have tacked right so he begins screaming, "More right More right!" To his credit, the guide wants us to catch a fish, but now he's starting to grate. In Spanish and English, I begin contradicting him; when he yells out, "Left!" I yell, "Right!" Now I can't help it, I start messing with him, saying the opposite, just to break up the monotony: "Left!" "Right!" "Left!" "Right!" "*¡Izquierda!*" "*¡Derecha!*"

Finally we have a good laugh and yes, even the guide mellows out a bit and laughs. (The joys of knowing Spanish. We're also good tippers.) In spite or because of the guide we had a great day of fly-fishing. Tom and I caught four different species of fish. The waters were simply alive with fish combat. At one point, I caught a jack crevale and just as I was bringing him into the boat, a barracuda, in an amazing burst of energy, jumped up and bit him in half. He left me reeling in the head.

That same afternoon, as we skirted a mangrove inlet, I spied what looked like an entire reef of conch. I had to take a break on land and check it out. Just a few steps out of the water I was amazed to see a huge bed of conchs. They were alive and crawling. Hundreds of healthy specimens with beautiful pink and reflecting shells. A large iguana stared at me across the conch bed.

I felt like that kid, so long ago, exploring wonderful nature all around me. A world so rich in life and color and variety. Every kind of bird—some of the birds were pink—feet, feathers, beaks and all. I wondered if it had to do with their diet, brine shrimp and all. I felt a strange oneness with the conchs. Standing there, looking around at this complex life system of roots and water, iguanas, birds, the sea, the sun. I could understand why the conch all gathered here at this beautiful spot. *I must be dreaming*, I said to myself.

TOM MCGUANE

Tom McGuane (born December 11, 1939) is a great American novelist, screenwriter and essayist. Early work shows him exploring picaresque experience in his unique literary style—novels such as Ninety-two in the Shade and Panama. During a spell in Hollywood, he wrote the screenplay for the classic film, The Missouri Breaks. Recent novels include, The Cadence of Grass and Driving on the Rim. Tom McGuane is an enthusiastic outdoorsman and has written perceptively about fishing (The Longest Silence), raising horses (Some Horses) and life in nature (An Outside Chance). He is a member of the American Academy of Arts and Letters, The National Cutting Horse Association Hall of Fame and the Flyfishing Hall of Fame. He has made Montana his home since the late 1970s.

Russell's Fish Index

TARPON (*pictured on the right*) Insane jumper; fast, one hundred yards in less than a minute; lovely silver fish; armor-plated mouth. Take him on the fly, that's the only way. Has beautiful scales, big as sand dollars. (pictured on right)

NEEDLEFISH Big around as the fat end of a baseball bat and five feet long. Needle sharp teeth; you don't really want to catch them; just pull your fly up quick, they're fast.

PUFFERFISH They are not usually all puffed out with spikes but, frightened, they will blow up big as a basketball. Marlin love them. Don't bother eating them, they are off the chart poisonous.

BONEFISH Silver, big pink lips; takes a small shrimp or crab fly pattern. Don't waste your time cooking them, terrible fare. Super-fast, they just take off, fun as hell; spooks fast. You have to sneak up on them.

CREVALLE JACK Platinum, strong fighter; I hooked into a fifteen pounder, a barracuda bit him in half, like a perfect cut from a scimitar.

RED SNAPPER Delicious; enjoyed catching them on the mantis prawn fly. Real mantis prawn kill more than they get eaten; red snapper love them. Hold on tight, they'll run to the bottom rocks and coral heads; snap your line.

COWFISH Nothing there, party's over. The bone structure is massive and you can't eat them. They say that everything in the ocean is edible but coral and sponges; I would throw in cowfish (don't send a recipe, I'm not going to try it!).

GROUPER They grow big, behemoth-sized; some say they grow as big as a Volkswagen bug. If you catch a big one, don't kill it. Stunningly delicious. One of my favorite food fish.

Black Beans & Rice

1 cup rice

3 cups dry black beans

9 cups water

1 yellow onion, diced

4 garlic cloves, minced

1 Tablespoon ground cumin

1 bay leaf

1 teaspoon dry oregano

2 teaspoons sugar

2 tablespoons olive oil for sautéing

1 lime, juiced

Russell's Original Seasoning, 2 Tablespoons +

Soak the beans overnight. The next day, drain the beans and set them aside while you sauté the onion. Once the onion has started to caramelize, add the beans, garlic, bay leaf, and oregano. Add water and boil for about half an hour to 45 minutes. Add rice and another cup or two of water. Allow to continue cooking until rice and beans are tender. Once the beans are cooked tender, add your seasoning, lime juice, sugar and let the beans stand off heat for ten minutes.

CHEF'S NOTE

This is a fantastic leftover dish the next morning. Sauté and add eggs. Roll in warm tortilla shells and eat.

Thank You

The people named below are all a part of my life and have helped me in some way. I want to offer a sincere thanks to them for believing in me. Thank you, thank you, thank you! And, to those others—you know who you are...thank you for all of the life adventure opportunities.

All of my staff over the years	*Bjorne Hansen*	*Patti Payne*
Doug Anderson	*Glenn Hart*	*Danielle Peterson*
Steve & Connie Ballmer	*Pete & Leslie Higgins*	*Jarda Ruzicka*
Stan & Alta Barer	*Laura Huston*	*Gerard & Jody Schwarz*
Kurt Beardslee	*Gunnar & Heidi Ildhuso*	*Dale Sherrow at*
Frank Bothwell &	*Jean Jorgensen*	*Seattle Caviar*
Linda Becker-Bothwell	*Ira Kaplan*	*Janis Taylor*
Charles & Barbara Burnett	*Scott & Patti Lennard*	*Chris & Barb Telge*
Chris & Tracee Chelios	*Tom McGuane*	*Eddie Vedder*
Mark Edson	*Bruce & Jean McNae*	*Terry & Lara Vehrs*
Karie Engels	*George & Peggy Lewis*	*Larry Votta*
Bill & Melinda Gates	*Felipe "George" & Becky Nunes*	*Iridio Photography &*
Kirke & Barb Lisi	*Tom O'Keefe*	*Darren Emmens*

CREDITS

Kelly Galloup of Slide Inn Trout Fly Fishing Lodge www.slideinn.com for the photo of the Zoo Cougar fly

Brian O'Keefe for the photos of Cuba

Montana Fish, Wildlife and Parks for the bear identification photos

Passio Creative